LATE BLOOMER,
LATE BLOOMER,
LATE BLOOMER

JAMES T. YOUNG

Contents

A Hang Up

As Eileen and I were driving back from our Christmas jaunts with our respective folks, she fell asleep, while I had a recollection. About thirty years back, as an estimate, after the co-op was built It became a place that our family traveled to from our hometown Of Greenwich to stay at when we went to the Mad River valley to ski. The name "co-op" was used to describe the place to others and for ourselves. It was named by a buddy of mine who lived in the condo right next to our unit. And my father George approved the slogan/name because his college bookstore at Yale is called the coop. There are five family second homes to the co-op and we certainly put it to use.

My sister with the coffee shop and a job as a phlebotomist lived there with her husband when she first got married, and I stayed there from time to time on the weekends when I went to the nearby university. My brother still uses the place to go skiing, and he goes skiing a lot, so during the "on season" the place is rarely vacant. When I became an adult, I had the idea in my head to spend all my time at the co-op, but then I suffered that first psychotic episode there. I wasted my days in listening to album music records, my head was spinning around like it was on the turntable but I wasn't aware of my state of health until the buddies' mom Eileen who was a certified Mental health nurse recommended me to seek guidance. Earlier in 1968 one summer at the co-op, Dad decided we were going to canoe down the Winooski River. We all packed into our white Pontiac, and with a canoe strapped to the roof, we drove from Fayston north towards a section of the river that ran north–south in the middle of the state. We had no itinerary other than canoeing down the river, but my mother and sister were prepared to pick us up with the Pontiac somewhere downstream (if we happen to make it that far). Cell phones hadn't been invented, so call us crazy, but we only had a general idea of where we'd rendezvous on a map.

The same as the family women. The day of the river run was warm and sticky, and we put the canoe in the river and began paddling like madmen, or at least my brother and father did. I didn't have to paddle, as I was only about 9 years old at the time. I sat in the middle of the canoe, a little apprehensive about going downriver. My brother paddled from the bow and my father from the stern. They synced up okay enough with the paddling. The side banks of the river, I could see clearly, were full of bushes, lined with trees, and high, with narrow openings made by the streams that entered and exited the river. My father was in his element, on the water, always the second ensign lieutenant on a USS Navy destroyer, even if we were just in a small canoe. I enjoyed the scenery, but despite the hot and humid weather. We were rounding a bend when suddenly my brother called out, "I hear rushing water, steer to the side bank!" What lay ahead in the Winooski was a massive 100-foot drop waterfall. We had no idea there'd be any obstacles to deal with on the river. I thought we were goners. My heart must have been pounding hard as a jackhammer, as my brother and my father steered as sharply and as strongly as a magnet seeking its polar opposite toward the bank and began to paddle furiously backward. The three of us grabbed for any stalk, weed, leaf, branch, reed, or blade of wild grass we could reach and threw our paddles up and onto the shore. Then we scrambled out of the canoe onto the riverbank. The winooski has many streams flowing in all different directions. On a map it looks like a brain's neuron cell. At first we were stumped over our next move. There was a lot of gear in the canoe and it couldn't be moved very far and we certainly couldn't wouldn't—go back the direction we came (and no cell phones, remember?). I could see the eyes of my father, the US Navy lieutenant suddenly burn, as he wasted no time in ordering us to hoist the canoe out of the water onto the shore. First problem solved. Now there was the problem of how we were going to get the canoe back into the water, but below the falls. I didn't know if these falls had a name and I hadn't seen Fitzcarraldo as yet, but in order to solve this coming dilemma, we'd have to portage the full canoe over a small, but scrubby mountain. What my father did next amazes me to this day. Little did I know that he had set out with his sons prepared with a winch, which we then used, via the length of rope my father had also thought to bring, to hoist and drag the canoe to the top of this big hill.

We couldn't have carried the canoe, anyway. Lowering the canoe downhill on the other side and gliding it to the water below was relatively easy. With great breaths of relief we jettisoned the canoe back into the Winooski and paddled onward. The river below the falls was not smooth. Many rapids and rocks had to be avoided.

About a mile down the stretch we managed to get the canoe wedged between two boulders, which invited river water to start rushing in and the canoe to wedge. My feet got soaked and moss-filled, and we started to lose everything in the canoe to the buoyant waters. It wasn't what I'd call a collision, as the rapids were shallow ones, but it still wrecked us enough that we had to right the canoe and collect as much of the floating equipment and provisions as we had hands for. The last leg of the journey smoothed out, with easing rapids and the paddling itself actually becoming as pleasant as the passing scenery. Before we paddled through this last stretch, we found one of my brother's missing shoe floating belly-up downriver! At the bridge we had generally mapped as our final destination, I finally saw my mother and sister waiving down at us, smiling as if we'd been through some leisurely day floating around under the sunshine. Seeing them was one of the most welcoming sights I have ever seen. I have never been happier to see a couple of women, nor happier to have seen much else since.

New Friends

Music is what feelings sound like.

Amen to that. My new resolution for the coming day was to resist any temptation of the greedy places out in society. I am saying it silently to myself, but with wholehearted conviction. I hoped for Eileen to be a girlfriend. The short blond hair she had and wonderful housekeeping ethics really attracted me to her. It was a beginning. I met Eileen through my other friend, my housemate, Jamal. She is his sister–in–law's best girlfriend. The place I live in at present is Spring Lake Ranch in Springfield, Massachusetts. Dad lives in Greenwich Connecticut with his wife, Helen. Dad's a very prominent attorney, and a hard act to follow. A tall man, and a navy second lieutenant ensign, he rescued me from a near disaster as a boy when I was picked me up like a feather because my buddy's fishing hook (same co-op buddy: son of Eileen) and line caught me in an eyelid while trout fishing in Fayston. The office of Dr. Quinby operated on me. He backed out the fishhook from my eyelid. To this day, I am lucky to see out of both eyes. I like hobbies that are going well. Photography, Plaster of Paris sculptures, and some paintings of acrylic. My father once told me, "Hobbies can be like digging for gold." It was sort of true in a couple cases when one painting I created was displayed at my college's alumni weekend and another was sold at the Bauch Arts Council Art Sale. I have no formal art instruction or training, but those pieces happened to come out well. So my father was not talking about fools gold, especially in a small awarded way. Here inside a government assisted house and Tony is also constantly at his drawing hobby. He's damn good at it, but gold? I had a lucky strike with mine. Tony is one of three other roommates. Tony has a girl of 35 named Dawn.

On one snowy wintery day, I heard the other housemate from downstairs announce, "It is another day for a snow removal job!" Jamal, a Far East Indian, slim, with a coffee-colored complexion, who acclimated quickly to Adult (with all its horrid vices(turned to me) "Jamie, why don't you be a better artist, a new hobby and do more work?" I, Jamie, am a tall, average body size Caucasian with a rather smooth, good looking face and a little smile. "I am exuberant about the day and I am ready to do something really productive, Jamal," I say, and end up shoveling snow and raking icy leaves for the house because no one else was around. They just decided to smoke cigarettes. Later, I decided to walk through the snowy afternoon to shovel more snow in downtown Springfield, and it was going to be on the city of Springfield's dime, because they were going to pay all of us. I had already prepared a warm set of clothing for the drop off of some film at the local drugstore due to awful weather. I also had to because The photos were important to me. "It looks like a blizzard.

It's gonna snow and keep on snowing!" I exclaimed jubilantly to the other shovelers, after I quit exclaiming and finally got to shoveling. The city's snow shoveling operation, if you can call it that, was run by a company that hires the disabled, the homeless, or just about anybody with two arms that happens to walk in asking for work. The snow finally stopped, and by then we had cleared the sidewalks. Before we were shuttled home, we went inside a small shelter to put away our equipment, took off our heavy gear, and drank some hot chocolate. Soon after I arrived back home, Tony said, "I'll do these dishes after I smoke a butt or two." Right, Tony, I thought to myself. Most of the residents hate doing their chores as much as Tony does. We have to do a lot of work voluntarily, elsewise the place would be a pigpen. Would Tony rather live in a pigpen? I did my own chores of putting away my laundry and organizing my desk, then said to Jamal, "Jamal, I want to get out of this group setting and get a place where I can at least manage my own phone and get a car." "We have to move forward," Jamal retorted. "I agree. Hey, you just picked some things out of the garbage, right?" "Yeah, so?" "You didn't mean to throw them away, did you?" I had thrown away some mail from the Black Otter Guide Service of Pray. Pray is a small town in the big sky country out west. "I do discard mail and then I regret it," I said. "Jamal—hey Tony!—these Black Otter outfitters are offering wilderness vacations in Pray." I had worked on a dude ranch out there in Pray years ago as a college boy pretending to be a cowboy, and I had already taken that "wilderness" vacation once. I did ride horses while I was there, and hunted rattlesnakes. There is a beaten-up public payphone in the foyer of the house, and suddenly it rang.

I didn't want to answer it, but I wanted it to stop ringing, so I picked up the receiver. Mistake. It was my dad, who had been really unpleasant lately. We didn't discuss much. He lectured me a bit about my less-than-adequate behavior at his house in the presence of his wife, Helen. My telephone card had very little time left on it so I quickened my goodbye to Dad and set the receiver back in place. Then one of the house counselors, dressed in a dapper woolen jumper and blue jeans, swung by on their scheduled monthly visit. "So Jamie, how are things going? I have some paperwork for you to sign. Just the goal plans for the coming months," he said. "You don't have to explain to anyone our situation here," I insisted. "I am taking my medication and we are all getting along fine here." Then I remembered what this counselor's superior, a woman who works at the agency and acts as our landlord, had said to me once: "Think about what you can do with what you hold." It was honest advice. It was late when the counselor finally left. "Goodnight, guys," I said. "Try not to go to bed too late, alright buddy?" "Good night, Jamie." Jamal said. The next day was frigid, and I was still forced to see a doctor. The state Medicaid transportation drives us to our appointments by taxi. This one's on Tumble Road. At the doctor's appointment, I talked mundanely about my day. Soon after I was taxied back to the residence, a woman, one subordinate social worker, arrived to check on me. "Did all you guys get your D work?" she asked. "D" work was necessary to make sure we were taking our Clozaril, the drug Jamal and I are taking. Jamal replied in the affirmative with a nod. "And you?" she says, turning to me. "Yes, I did." I answered. "Good," she said, with the authority of an ex-drill sergeant, because that is what she is. After she left and dusk fell, I said to Jamal and Tony, "Men, wouldn't this be a good time to go out and drink and party all night?" I try to emancipate myself in my mind, which I know sometimes appears right in the right timing, because its a barren and tense house where we all live crammed together. My mood is getting more comfortable here than when I first moved in. I know myself. I've been very spoiled due to my fill of recreations but I'm maturing, and thank God I am not lazy. I am really willing to work and put my best foot forward, but one issue persists— really just one, which is that I can be unfrugal, and my work is lazy. What I want is to get to an independent base where I can manage my own telephone charges, have a car, and a solid home, etcetera, etcetera. I try not to point fingers at either of my roommates. Instead I try to be diplomatic. But even then, the same compulsion persists. What I like to do most is get out at night and bar hop or gamble but taking that risk on my limited income would be completely bonkers. Oh well. Tony, Jamal, and I wake up on totally different schedules. I am usually up at five like Jamal is, but Tony as a rule sleeps until nine. Today, up at five as usual, Jamal and I will be riding to various locations to either shop or hunt for work on the county bus. We traveled to west Springfield and stopped at a diner. "Jamal," I said. "Could you order me cereal and a black coffee?" "Why don't you order your own? You're sitting here just like me," Jamal retorted. The problem was, instead of thinking about breakfast, I was thinking about my sister,

Gloria. "Sorry, Jamal, today is my sister's birthday. October 27!" For some reason, I ended up announcing this to everyone in the diner. No one even looked up. "Oh yeah? How old is your sister?" Jamal asked. "Fifty," I said, thinking to myself, I will call her on the payphone later if I still have enough credits. It would be better talking to Gloria than to my Dad that was for sure. I'd been angry with dad. Jamal offered to order for us, and I ate my cereal and drank my coffee plus a refill, and we paid the check. The rest of the day in west Springfield was fruitless job hunting. I walked in and out of businesses and shops, until the quick in-and-outs became as boring a routine as sitting at my desk and trying to write. At least the latter brought some satisfaction. I'll have a diploma degree (needing 33 credits) but I never focused on one area, so I know it will be very hard to get a decent paying job, much less a career, with my skeletal skill set and very general, even vague, education. My father dwarfs me with his successes, as he always finds ways to remind me. Yet I persist in running around in the sub-zero temperatures and even colder wind chill factor looking for something that will probably never come. I always believed everyone should have the know-how and necessary skills to shop for a job, but researching for hope of a job is a full-time job unto itself, and it's a job that doesn't pay. Go figure. I resent my minimal economic budget, but I have to get used to it and stop being so obsessed with my finances, because it's an obsession over nothing. Nada. I was getting disheartened and exhausted, so, as a fantasy, I rode the local bus to different local merchants and priced out the things I'd like to buy, but the reality killed the fantasy that sent me into the shops, some of which were the shops I had just stepped in and out of asking for work. It was sheer madness and somewhat a frustration. Jamal reappeared from around the corner and back from his own efforts and met me at the bus stop and we headed back to the Community residence. As I had stood around in the cold, waiting for buses and job offers that never came, even after all the ins and outs at the shops, the idea struck that I ought to try to reach my brother Harold at our co-op, since it happened to be a few hours away from Springfield. Back when the family chalet served as a happy vacation home for all of us, I remember the two of us listening to the 1967 hit by The Turtles, "Happy Together."

Harold and I always talked about this song in particular because it portrayed how easygoing our family life had been. After that, we ended up buying lots of music from that era. 5 Another group he and my co-op neighbor, Paul, turned me on to was a book about The Doors entitled, No One Here Gets out Alive. Every reason I couldn't really bed down at the chalet, even if Harold did happen to answer in the present, was because my father had willed it to him, not me, and because some legal clause states that no one can live there year-round.

* * *

The residence we all live in is called Spring Lake Ranch, a multi-story house that sits amid some wooded mountains. I ended up here because I had to get away from home, and soon. I have a small room in the house, and the house has two floors and sits in the center of a huge lawn. My room is upstairs, and there are three beds in it, one for me, one for Jamal, and one for Tony. The three of us are sitting around when we hear a loud buzz. "Is that your laundry in the machines down in the basement?" "Yes," I replied. "The machine just buzzed," he said. "Yeah, I heard." The buzz signals that the wash is over. "Why aren't you going to get it?" I stand up. "I am." As I descended to the basement to gather my clothes and throw them in the dryer, I thought, what with how cold and furious the winter was becoming outside, how great it was to be so warm and cozy and protected inside. When I returned to the room, I said to Jamal and Tony, "It's going to be a bleak winter, men, but I happen to like snow." They continued to relax on their beds in front of the television. "I only wish I had tax refunds coming in April, so I'd have some cash, but that won't happen," I said. Jamal and Tony smirk. "The truth is I haven't held down a job in my life." My goals for living here at the Ranch have become to learn how to handle a vocation and become independent, and also how to stabilize my upward mobility, keep my feet working, and my moods stable. I had yet to realize my lazy work ethic. So far, I've only become less fickle about things, though I want to become good and lively. I still feel like I have scarcely lived. "Are you glad I moved in with you two?" I sometimes ask my housemates, usually to no response. Soon after meeting one another here, we became fast friends and ended up staying together in one room, Jamal, Tony, and me. Maybe it's because the three of us agreed that life in this dog eat-dog, bloody hell of a world offered nothing definite besides "death and taxes," the refrain that both my uncle and father also always passed along. Were we all here for the same psychosis troubles, in regards to our present scenario and situation? The next day the weather was cold, but the sky had turned blue. "Tell me about some of your relationships," the counselor asked me in my mandatory session, to which I sheepishly replied, "My love life is good. All along, I hoped to possibly date this girl, Eileen, but she never let me in (like her heart) Maybe because my grandiose expectations failed her before I even had the chance to be in a relationship with her. Now I have a girlfriend. Though it is not smoothly going along." "So what have you been doing with your time?" the counselor. "I carry my bag around with me looking at everything just like I did when I was a teenager. I don't have paid work, but I try to keep healthy. I don't excessively eat or smoke, and I keep up with my end of the chores around the residence, while the other guys surely don't." "I see. Well, all I can say, is 'good for you.' It's a start, right?" "I guess," I say, choosing not to bother her with any of my preferred evening misadventures or my "true" feelings. But maybe I should start—hell, I spend most of my evenings alone without sneaking into mischief so how is an earlier talk with my therapist going to be able to do that? And it is unlikely that I am able to get out at nights with no transportation. Like my Dad if he were in business rather than law: Before I even chance to attempt that, my psyche first has to become more positive. The writing helps, but progress is slow, and these days I spend more time keeping focused by cleaning and eking out my minimal life according to its minimal economic budget.

Basically, I am doing what I am told to do, trusting that one day some good will come of it. And the work I am told to do around the Community residence in Spring Lake

Ranch never ceases. Everyday there are dishes to wash and dry and clean and polish, and thank God for the dirty dishes, as they keep my mind scrubbed and clear, especially with some of the health problems encroaching upon me these recent year—prostate cancer, acid reflux, "GERD," as they call it. After seeing my counselor, I reunited with Jamal and Tony in our room. Jamal's already hypnotized by the television. "My dad and I have a long-distance relationship, but we have a good father-son bond," I tell Tony, trying to disguise my still manifesting college spoilage. "Oh yeah?" Tony cracks back. I doubt he even heard me. Each day, I spend some hours on the house computer, though I never receive many emails. What I do most is practice web design through a free library service. I prefer to go to the library to do any printing I have to do, and it's a short trip so I usually walk, at least there, and usually take the bus back. Every time I leave for the library, Tony, like human clockwork, asks, "Where are you going?" "You know where I am going, Tony," I always say. Does he really give a rat's ass, I don't know. It doesn't matter. Once, on the way home, the bus broke down and everyone had to exit so I ended up walking back home, too. Could you believe the bus had an oil leak and everyone took out their lighters and lit up butts anyway? Some people. All this time so far at the residence, I have been going to "program"—rehabilitation therapy. I hate attending group activities, "therapeutic" or otherwise. People always appear so grumpy, always try to sneak away for a smoke, or try to borrow, beg, or steal, while everyone else is stuck complaining in a circle. e.g. "Are there no concrete rules to adhere to?" Jamal once asked out of the blue on the program "Jamal," I said, casting a sideways glance at him. "Do whatever you want, just be good." Everyone nodded. "I am always good," Jamal finally answered. "Well, as we go," I said, and some people laughed, this guy from the residence next door, Neil, and I sometimes went for walks at the nearby park, mainly to get away from the Community Residence in the evening and because he and I were the most athletic—though I still don't regard walking as a particularly athletic activity. I guess some do. Before I could get to know Neil beyond our walks, he had moved back with family, or at least his brother. I can't go back to my family, but I can still at least go to my brother's house outside the state at Thanksgiving to eat a nice turkey dinner.

What a mistake I made, getting myself into this incendiary world. I have no nuclear nor extended family left and I miss that. I face every day now, miraculously trying and there are struggles that come with every dawn. But the situation I found myself in at that college was horrific, with no money for car, rent etc and no job to do, while my father was preoccupied, mother having just passed away....It was a tough time, and it makes the rehab fix look wonderful nobody really cherishes a rehab until possibly nor bad times but When Upward mobility begins, physics will say things in motion tend to stay in motion while things at rest tend to stay at rest What a pipe dream, I have no independence and I miss that. It would be nice to be served and taken care of ie. looked after, dad, my brother and sister, all together as a family again, instead of dealing with the impersonal reality I face every day now, and the remorse that comes with it. It's no longer my birthday every day, the cake and ice cream are gone, the candles and wishes blown out. I no longer slurp life from an economic-filled silver spoon. So what happens for a single man and no companions. I try to witness and watch with my mind: (a movie from time to time.) Ahh it was relaxing to watch a movie today, The Big Chill, and it has been a year since I was admitted.

No Longer Adhesive Therapy

Consider it most unlike myself to be a heathen to a spouse or life partner. If I'm ever with someone, I'll stay away from nighttime endeavors and places of appetites like clubs and bars. The problem has always been that I lacked the financial confidence required for attracting a spouse. Today, life doesn't come cheap or easy. One either "pays ass one goes" or pays over their entire life. It is a choice. Either way, you pay. There isn't much of a social outlet if there's no money. I always sided on recreation aspects of socializing.

Today I took the bus straight through Springfield and went to the Clubhouse, the Ranch's workplace for people with psychiatric or financial or literacy difficulties, and that day at the Clubhouse, I had breakfast. I was hoping to see Eileen there when I walked in but she wasn't there to meet me. It is already "hump" day: Wednesday. At the Clubhouse, I did some computer viewing and continued with my study and practice of web design. I was always good with computers, so I should probably carry on with it. Programming is what I did best, but that was a long time ago. Programming is what I think I should carry on with most. It required a lot of brainpower, and probably requires even more today. Or maybe not. Who really knows? I enjoy programming because it combines numbers into a language all its own. The languages I spoke best were Basic and FORTRAN, which I studied for one semester at school. I went back to the residence at lunch and I looked through my mail. I received a letter from Helen:

Dear Jamie,

This is the check that belongs to you. Please deposit it into your bank and please think several times before you spend it. I will speak to you soon.

Love,
Helen

I was up early one Saturday morning in our second-floor room. Winter is not officially over. There are signs of spring. Suddenly it is very warm. Outside the sun is shining and there is blue across the sky and the days are getting longer. Birds chirp, some blue jays have arrived. I was looking out the windows of our room and saw a red-winged blackbird flying in a flock of common grackles. I love birds. I feel a lot better with people equal in brains to me, and the CR in Spring Lake Ranch definitely gets me to brain up. All of us here at the residence have to see doctors, go to programs, and carry the "estranged" label or a stigma. But there's a warm feeling in the house, and, as I say, I have three hots and a cot. And to have three hot meals and a bed to sleep on. For now, that's enough. Living with others in close quarters requires care, respect, attention, and doing what you are told. Everyone has to listen to someone else at some point in their lives, right? Every day, I restart myself and I won't give up. Unlike Tony, who doesn't seem to care and will never be able to listen to anyone. He's already given up. I don't know how he'll ever restart himself. The counselors have been encouraging me to join another program, the town's other rehabilitation therapy, Day Treatment Center, but it was President's Day, so my new program interview was moved forward a day. When I met the program directors the following day, I was denied lunch at the interview because I am not yet a member. My struggles had me offkey because my peers from schooling and a stay in the U.K. were my recreation fellows and women while these residents were alternates "It was an awful place to spend a day," Jamal had told me. "The clinic does not do anything productive," Tony had interjected. Whatever. I'll make my own decisions. I dislike their grumpy plight, all their smoking all the time, and their always borrowing whatever can be borrowed. I considered this day a good day because at least I got a chance to go over my résumé with a certified social worker. I just like to write, I whispered to myself. The résumé will allow me to find employment even though I don't have a car. For some reason, I see my résumé as the key to one day entering my family dream home, not the old family home, but a new one buzzing with a new family. Today is Ash Wednesday and I was just at Yale-NewHaven Hospital in near Greenwich visiting my Dad. He just had a knee replacement, so he was walking with a cane. At the hospital there was a church service. Just being with my

Dad offers the best Christian religion can offer me because it is pinpointed (as Jesus Christ) and not so generally cosmic like Buddhism: Just to see my dad walking and alive brought a grin. "I am really happy to see you Dad," I told him. After seeing my dad, I took the Greyhound bus back to Spring Lake Ranch. It was a foggy and rainy Monday morning and the start of a new week. It never feels too exuberant on a cloudy Monday morning but I gave it my best shot. Again I walked to the local library. It was pouring rain, but I felt at ease and comfortable inside, out of the pouring rain. I arrived at the library a little shy of its 9:30 a.m. opening. After I entered, I went to the civil service preparation exams room and researched what it would take for me to earn a certificate and take the civil service exam to become a social worker. I was feeling a bit heavily medicated.

Later, after I got back to Spring Lake Ranch, I was doing dishes in the kitchen when i completely abated the interest in applying for the social work exam. Because I can never keep up with a position of employment! It's because of a resume at an earlier age?, It's because I never had much of a work ethic and my skills are minimal. But if there is a will, there is a way. What I need is a "can do" attitude. Friday brought daydreaming along my walk as I was again visiting the open library's entrance doors and everything turned into a sort of trip. It reminded me of the hallucinations of LSD trips. To describe this illicit, horrific street drug Jamie says, "My mind seemed condensed, tight. As a reaction, I turned up "Peace of Mind" by the band Boston (remember them?) on my Walkman, and my immediate world slowly started to slow."

Music

Is What Feelings Sound Like?

"If music is the food of love, play on!" This is a quote of my father's which has also come to fruition for me. Once, in a counseling session, I blurted out, "Once, in a while my mind and my mood caves in at times." I always want to make friends, but if the 'friends' use me, I'd rather not be near them. I'd prefer to have a friendship with my co-op neighbor, Paul." He was a childhood buddy for the longest time. What is hard in life is to break out of circles of old friends and start anew. And Paul is my fishing buddy's brother.

There was that one day I skipped program, and walked to the stores in the downtown Springfield mall with the grandiose idea of buying myself some clothes—or at least I wished of buying certainly didn't have the money for myself, because while I was walking inside the mall by the stores dreaming about buying clothes, I remembered Eileen asking me to give her a call. I did so on one of the newest technology advances in our time A cell phone that is out on the market. I decided to have my eyes examined, even though I already had a pair of glasses I received through my Medicaid benefits. I couldn't afford to buy a pair for myself that day. (Though years later, I would buy glasses with better, more stylish frames for $100.) When you leave and return to a place a lot, you start to notice things. Lately, there has been a lot more peace in the house. I'm getting settled and people seem to like me more. At dinner, Jamal asked, "Are you going to the Halloween party?" "No," I replied. "I just telephoned Eileen to ask her out on a date at Clubhouse for Halloween." "Yo," said Jamal. "I am going to watch television now!" What else is new, I thought. It was nasty outside, so after dinner I watched the movie, Harry Potter and The Deathly Hallows. The end of the film depicted how fighting good spirits overcame the bad souls and spirits (bad spirits below the animal kingdom), somewhere there in Hell. It was great, though I had already read the book of the same name a while ago. I arrived back to our dead asleep house after a hard day of riding around to different locations all day. Really tough life! Some days the buses are late and sometimes they don't even arrive. Later that night, I called Eileen back with some bad news (she had left me a message on my cell phone). "Eileen, I don't have the money to take you to the Clubhouse party, and to tell you the truth, I am a little frightened by it. So how about you go to the residence Halloween party with me?" "Sure," she said. We said goodbye to each other, and I hung up. I just love how simple, genuine, and agreeable Eileen is. I spied Jamal over in his corner behind the television, "Looks like I will be going to the party after all," I said. The Sunday was getting lazier so my roomies and I went to our room to relax, until Tony opened his mouth. "I have bad memories of the hospital I was in about a year ago," he said. "It was a V.A. hospital." Jamal became quiet. Any trace of mental illness frightens him. And I know how bad I felt about my hospital visit years ago. Some talk a lot to shift their attitude, Jamie is active in both mind and body, but Jamal is still a bit of a foreigner, so doesn't talk like Tony does. He's still outside that sphere of influence.

The residence Halloween party was a huge success, and my anniversary. Halloween was the very day I first moved into Spring Lake Ranch to start my long journey to independent living. There were many unique costumes, a lot of comic heroes, some civil war reenactors—and the best costume I saw was a man swimming around looking like a big trout fish. It was the best Costume of the night party and Eileen commented and agreed on it. This was better than sitting in front of a TV all the time. It is tiring and makes me sick. I should have signed up for ROTC but I didn't. I am a good candidate for this rehabilitation agency that I live in. It reminds me of what it must have been like being a settler living in an old homestead, mostly because of the continual exercise of chopping wood. I'm getting the right education to advance, but I know full well that jobs requiring only the use of brains are rare indeed, so I guess getting fit is an added bonus here. Chopping wood offers just such a bonus. If I wanted to be a computer programmer, but so far I've only taken one class with some FORTRAN thrown in. I didn't get enough education in computers, so it is difficult to learn, but if you want to be in business, you have to produce, work with both hands and put your back into your work, basically speaking. My father, God bless him, is a lawyer, but unlike "like father like son," I just went through the motions of my education, never focusing on any particular career.

The work that Tony does is fairly simple, some assembly business where he doesn't take home much money. Jamal, well, Jamal, when he's not glued to the TV, just socializes at the Clubhouse. My real desire is to go fully kinetic with a job so I can finally have money. I'll have a college degree one day, but the jobs I dream about are too lofty for my qualifications. New college graduates shouldn't aim so high, especially grads with low GPAs like mine. I want to be rich—right now—without working hard for it. But that's not impossible: Tony feel's the same, and Jamal, we never know what he wants. The way I feel about the present is that we are all in a coerced situation. Its just improbable knowing that once we save $2000 dollars or more they will deny us our disability income and benefits. I take each day in this situation with a renewed future principle in mind. As much as I sneered at my school teachers, I'll sneer, even hate, any future bosses I have even more. This is a pseudo-abhorrence, obviously, because I am not the belligerent sort, in fact I have learned to become content among mankind. Today, I'd get tired of any productive work they throw at me. All I want to do is kick back and relax after the work week with a weekend calendar of football. Some more veteran residents than me have had five or six years of this scene they call a "home" for people with psychiatric afflictions. How do they do it? Beats me. "When does this shit get any better?" asks Tony, and then starts to sing. Tony loves to sing, unfortunately he's bad, as he starts to hum some vague rock-and-roll (?) song.

The best-laid road to my success must steer clear of the vices and money traps in society.

This includes drinking establishments, clubs, lottery, and horse betting, etcetera, etcetera. Thank God I don't have a smoking habit like so many others here—it would cost me a ten dollar note every other day. At least I'm developing a good base of true friends, I think, and I have a girlfriend (or do I?),. I think about money traps a lot. One important credo I repeat to myself is to never leave anywhere without some cash on your person. Jamie has so many times gone bust and just crashed on the bed, with nothing to show but a night shot to hell, and the promise of a better day to come rendered useless. Forty dollars on hand or a couple of thousand in the bank, I'll never have enough monetary staying power to rent my own place. Not yet, maybe not ever. I am a big spender, I don't crave new things, I just need to grow up and get my entity screwed on straight. These days, with the Internet and personal computers, it's easy to keep watch over where my money goes through online banking. Growing up as part of the family of a highly touted lawyer who, for some reason, never discussed law, nor his constant, daily war, but always discussed investments, I kind of, very kind of, followed suit and now preoccupy myself with wishful investment thinking. Changing that won't do me any good. But, common sense, now that's a willful philosophy I can own that can uniquely make me stand out in this crowded, competitive world.

I've always dealt pretty well with peer pressure but now I've reached the age that I don't pressure myself to keep up with my buddies' or the "Joneses'" activities. Now that I don't have much work, I have a lot of free time to devote to the activities so, ironically, I have more free time. I'd like to pursue… School is out now, except for studies of the personal kind. My father had been prepaying my college until my mother passed away and my safety net collapsed, and down I spiraled down straight into a mental hospital. After 11 months of being locked away there, I was released and fled the sway of my father into Spring Lake Ranch. Now that I've picked up the pieces here, I am finally able to hold a job, and have gathered enough skills and funds to meet some of the challenges of independent living. George allotted me to finish college.

He had such a magnanimous heart, my old man. But my father was a staunch conservative, so I was reared so naively and controlled as to be told "you can't smoke". The old friends fanned out across the continent and new friends who live locally, even right next to me, well this is an expansion of living a livid lifestyle and trying to make a living. The psychiatrists were a great help initially, but after one endures months, then years of boring therapy, one discovers that the doctor is just another mentor we pay to talk to. Talking is important, but you can talk to anybody, can't you? Taking the right medications, especially without combining them with drink, is very important, but is a lonely road indeed. The residence's social workers visit monthly, but there are also traveling companions we can utilize if we so desire. I plan on making good use of them (I'd rather travel with Eileen) until I get a mix of people around me who can tell what the hell is really wrong with me. James quotes, "I am a utopian sort with Vertigo." A men's group that we could form would be helpful. The monogamous groups don't help as the age-old adages supposedly do and one I particularly don't find is, "Quality attracts quantity in any organization." Tony and Jamal are my only close friends now.

Adjusting around/ Actively Seeking Work

"A lot of people, people with disreputable means and ways are still taking advantage of freedom riding the trains," I said "They are doing what?" asked Tony. "They get on the city train, then walk off at an earlier stop or offer another, old ticket at the ticket collection. But the Springfield bus suits me fine and it's only five-and-a-half dollars and gets me going where I need to go," I concluded.

Later in the day, I thought of planning (but I didn't go) to go by the Springfield bus to the high school track, visit Gloria, and run a lap, and maybe many more. I've been trying to become fit, though the reality is I'm 239 pounds, overweight, and not athletic at all. I wonder what it's like to be in super great shape. Must be nice. I just can't seem to get those great abs. While I was doing some calisthenics to warm up, I mentioned to Jamal, "If there are 440 yards in one lap, it only figures that four laps, one mile, is 5,280 feet." Jamal just stared at me, nodded, and turned back to the TV. He was watching the Jack LaLanne Show. In the middle of some jumping jacks, my eyes turned to the top of Jamal's dresser. There was a piece of chewed-up gum on it. What a mess. Later that day I rode into town on that five dollar-and–fifty cent bus. Now, after the clear sunrise, the stratus clouds that had started to streak the sky had darkened, threatening rain after a sunny morning. After some exercise, I was really out of breath, and only after a mile and some sit-ups I walked past a laundry shop with a "Help Wanted" sign taped to the window, so I went in and got an application. The only good thing about this type of work is that it'd be off the books.

Then I rode the return bus back on the same route. On the way in, I checked my mail. There was nothing. Back at home in my room, I tried to get my head together, working up a résumé and filling out the laundromat application. Jamal's old chewed gum had been cleared. I took the same bus back to deliver my application and résumé to the laundry proprietor later that day. Now the weather had turned fickle. The clouds were white and gray, and the sun was peeking from behind the clouds, so I figured it'd be a nice day. But then it began to drizzle. The laundromat was run by some Chinese people, and with my sentiments toward Buddhism, I decided to turn away. On the way home on the same bus, it began to pour rain. I said to myself, this is ridiculous, I can't ride a bus this far everyday for such a minor job, anyway! The back and forth was already spinning in my head. Imagine doing it every day! When I got home, I looked over some of my needed 33 college course listings and the dismal GPA that went before them. At least I had some college behind me. I decided I won't ever have to be involved with a laundromat. I had gone to this job's Help Wanted sign because it disgusts me that I often spend entire days at the residence just watching TV or sleeping (they are kind of the same, anyway). I know I picked up avoiding these habits from our family. What really gives me joy is keeping busy with diverse activities like studying foreign languages, learning how to program computers, keeping a diary, and working outdoors, especially raking leaves. Am I weird because I enjoy raking leaves? When I was a Boy Scout, I got my first taste at raking leaves and had a lot of fun playing in leaves at the Ivy League football tailgate parties that Dad took us to. Another activity that gives me a lot of joy is sneaking out at night to look up at stars in the night sky and match them up with a night sky map, so I can figure out their names. I can always spot Orion's belt and the Big and Little Dipper. Sometimes I read the Bible under the stars. One new constellation I spotted was the Hercules one, where he is half God and half man.

There was influenza going around in the community residence. I caught a flu bug and upchucked about three times. I stayed in bed the whole next day, getting up only to use the bathroom and drink water, and I drank plenty of that. It was disgusting, but it felt healthy to flush out the flu germs by throwing up. The flu had me fasting all week, and I didn't eat anything, not even one cracker. Even after all that, my flu got worse, and had me shitting so much diarrhea that I had to be taken to the ER and spend eight hours with an IV stuck into me because I had become so dehydrated. No wonder we are constantly told to get flu shots. The shit can kill you. (Along this time I would undergo knife prostate surgery after a diagnosis at Springfield Medical Center. That was also no joke. It made me incontinent for a spell. In order not to piss my pants, I had to retrain myself to go to the bathroom like a baby.) Finally, after about a week of being turned inside out by the flu, I am well again. Well enough to see my favorite girl Eileen again, a pretty heavyset woman with short blond hair. She and I went shopping at the mall so she could get her new prescription eyeglasses. We also bought some food and sat with it having a lunch break at the food court. Then we hung around town for about an hour and a half just browsing at clothes and walking—I didn't care much for that first time around, but it was a real kick talking that "puppy love" as we sense. I had my big love and my initial one. I wouldn't call it love. I was discovering that Eileen was not really too fond of me. That Socialist country at the time, on a four-month visa and my second job there was in a disco. Well, the bar manager set me up with a secretary, a twenty-year-old and it was a short fling, just enough to knock the gonads. But that was a long time ago. I won't go into the emotional bit because I think about it. Tonight, finally a Friday, I am feeling my old self again after being nearly killed off by the flu. And what did I do but watch a basketball game on TV. TV's fading from my agenda, and I almost never watch it anymore except to catch the latest weather report. I usually center my focus around weather because knowing it is essential if I am to work at landscaping, which I do in the warm weather months, and so make my usual runs back and forth into civilization and society, for a few neighbors. Now, while everyone else at Spring Lake Ranch CR is getting geared up for some eventual night party, I persist in making my runs to the library, stick with my therapy and counseling, and I am still single at 44 years of age. Bearing the label of stigma tells horrible tales. Every individual at Spring Lake Ranch bears the weight of their own social disease path and what has stigmatized them. All of us here have different issues and most of us are unaware of our ill emotions, but we embrace the diversity. Out of everyone, only Jamie—that's me—seems to know bookwise about himself. He has schizophrenia and narcissistic personality disorder. May be true, likely is true. I am handicapped in my head? No Only an growing attitude, but seems to have conquered the "Big Why," and is starting on the "Big How." I had also optimized a modicum of his feelings to bear an attitude of work and faith. Are these things fixed or variable, they hand in hand. It is likely, ill emotions are someone else in the picture too pretentious enough and surfaces in an individual. As much aloof as any teenager could muster, my years later became years of continual resilience. A plaque screwed to one of the walls of the residence states: ATTITUDE IS 90% OF LIFE. What the plaque might intend to say is: 90% of people hate to work. But at least I will try to and can be reliable and diligent to "the" company!" For all of us being so stigmatized, our meetings are very peaceful. They'd better be, because if we do harm to others or ourselves, the counselors will watch us pretentiously and recommend cautiously to hospitalize us immediately. The surrounding neighborhoods are separated from the Ranch, though sometimes their various inhabitants mingle. The family homes in the area seem quite unique to us community dwellers. Suddenly there is a nice stretch of blue-sky days. What a relief as we have had too much rain lately. I decided to take another trip, this time really to the Mad River

Valley. I took the Valley Transit. When I got to the depot, I called my counselor to check in and they recommended ways to tell me to turn back and not go. What? I felt a little bit insulted because this was a ridiculous recommendation. It was all because I missed a visit with my sister, Gloria, who was going to help me out with some money. Money is an ongoing worry of mine, and apparently of my counselors, and God knows who else—my old man? Everyone in my world seems to have the fear I will travel out somewhere and get stuck in a place with no money and no way home. I don't carry a credit card with a big balance, and my well-known tendency is to spend, spend, and spend some more. Mostly on a potpourri of stuff. This leaves me with very little for an emergency, so I suppose the concern is warranted. So, Jamie made it as far as the Depot and walked back but neglected his visit with his sister Gloria. A few days later, I received a letter from my brother, Harold:

Jamie

Everything is well here. No, we have not raked any leaves yet. I'm sure you were wondering. We are still trying to finish off some house painting, when the warm, dry days come. Unfortunately, there have not been too many of those recently. We'll probably do some raking here over Thanksgiving, although it's possible we may go to Grandma's instead. We'll find out tonight. I just found reading, Plum Island, by Nelson Demille. It is chock full of North Fork, Claudios, Old Town Tavern, The Vineyard, Orient, etc. If you haven't read it yet, I highly recommend it, although I suppose it is only considered a mandate for anyone who's ever lived in the east end residing there.

Yours,
Harold.

What I surmised from Harold's letter is that I can better his "want" lists with a travel book I have in which (specifically) Pray is highlighted as a good sight to see in the Big Sky State, and all the outlying escape towns across all the states in the country are, too. The book is Small Town Escapes, a National Geographic publication. In my present staged servility, where actual wanderlust is discouraged, my plan is to finalize my paradigm—not through psychology or education yet still treatment, but by working toward a goal. Like my brother Harold, Jamie has always been a good actor, but not a good soldier or "grunt." I did my best in my earliest schooling. I finished secondary school, and will finish college, at least without failing. I have been in group therapy, been hospitalized, been on serious medications. Fine, but it is work that has always "done it" or would "do it" for anyone whose somebody One work experience I had in the past was really exciting. In the past twenty years after I boarded away from my family home at 14 for four years of boarding school, which after I left, my Dad referred to it as a "country club." The tremendous job was working as a thrasher (taking up plots of wheat and barley) on the North Sea for four months in another Socialist country. That was super. Everything since then has been sort of a letdown. I spent a year in a mental hospital in "hatred" Hartford, and then worked at various sucky jobs like doing proofreading and being a payroll clerk in Hartford, as awful a town as I have ever been to.

While I was in this horrid excuse for a town, I was lucky to be taken out and moved to Springfield ranch and mentored closely back to good health by my stepmother, Helen, who assertively straightened out my personal and financial mess, donated her brain to my various illiteracies, or at least got me back on the right track. Now I'm in the kitchen sitting at the dining room table staring into the aquarium looking at fish and listening to the bubbles or the hum of the dishwasher and for some reason, it's easy to write. The kitchen is very smoky, so I open a window. I love fishing and in fact I am cooking fish that I just caught today. I like to fish for bluefish, and the ones I catch, I usually keep. Sunset Bluff has a great private beach for catching bluefish. If I feel like going fishing, I have to first ask. My aquarium contains five fish that I feed once a day. I snack a lot and I always go for milk and cookies, so when I feed myself, the fish always swim to the glass and longingly stare at me to also feed them. In the residence, the staff watches carefully that no one abuses privileges. It's a fine rule for me but some residents seem to overindulge of food. Probably out of boredom.

The 10-gallon tank is my release and nicely lights the room from its purple-lit aquarium stone. Speaking of light, I also have a fiber optic lamp that casts blue light. To my mind, fishing is one of the hobbies I do the best at. After cooking and eating the fish, I do a few things on my computer, including filling out surveys for a research firm. I also refer friends to sign up for a new solar energy program. If I make a referral, I get $25. I usually use the Web to get information or e-mail my brother, Harold, and his children. I also sell items on eBay and Letgo. So far, this is how I've put to use the computer knowledge I gained in that one college course. I head upstairs to the room I share with Tony and Jamal. Neither of them seems to notice how stuffy the room is, but I do, so I turn on the air conditioner.

When the mail arrives, I open a nice letter from my niece:

Dear Jamie,

I just thought I'd write a quick note to say hello and see how you are doing. I'm sure that you are working hard at your various jobs, you have a good work ethic since you started there, keep it up. Just remember to stay warm while you're working. I think it's going to be a cold winter. I'm starting a business with a friend. We are going to do catering with planning and decorating. When I set up my new business cards, I will send one to you. Well, take care and keep busy, enjoy life and keep in touch!

Your,
Karen

It is so like our family to say they're going to do something without ever actually doing it, so I wonder if my niece Karen will actually do what she says. I hope she does. Our father was really the sole one with the work ethic to accomplish things. My niece Karen is a successful secretary in a gastroenterologist's medical firm, but who do you think got her the position? My dad! What is hard is to be productive when your efforts go unrewarded. But I do enjoy the volunteer chores around the residence.

In fact, my father often told me you'd better appreciate your own labor resorts, because no one else will appreciate them for you. When I was not as busy as now, I always wrote, to either document my life at work or too validate my absence from a regular routine.

My attitude shines at the job of scrubbing the dirty bathtub and I enjoy work when I can learn new things. Someday I hope to be rewarded for my output. The Spring Lake Ranch staff insists we live in a clean environment, picking up after ourselves, clothes, dinner dishes, so on and so forth. This command is easy for Jamie, but not so universally accepted amongst the residents. The primary things that bother me about living with fifty other people in the same house is getting everyone else to get along without bickering, and, worse, that I have no private nook where I can be alone with my thoughts. That is why getting out into my own space has become my biggest goal. For now, with these minimal economic means, I can't live my preferred way. I just don't have enough funds to rent a place of my own, not yet.

Incendiary

A strange woman we'd never seen before came into the Spring Lake Ranch House and laid down on a bed. What she was doing there, I didn't know, but she shouldn't have been there. She was nobody's friend and unfamiliar, but if I had to describe her she had long dark hair with green eyes and was average height and good looking. When we spotted her— actually the staff spotted her, she freaked, "Get me the fuck out of here!" The scene itself was almost a crime. Sure enough, the police came and she reacted by locking herself in a Toyota Camry, which we assumed was hers, but soon found out was a resident's. What was funny to me was that we were in a "social interaction" setting and we couldn't even resolve this crisis without outside help. The fire department showed up, too, with their axes at the ready. She eventually got out of the car to explain to the police that she didn't want her son to have a car there. Go figure. The police left and we never really found out why she had to sneak in even if she didn't want her son to have a car at the Ranch. They must have had a responsible relationship and she simply wanted to punish him. Then one workday, after dinner, I was about to fall asleep when suddenly I heard Rosemary (one counselor) yelling and some commotion coming from the house adjacent to ours. Tony, Jamal, and I ran downstairs from our room and ran outside.

I got downstairs ahead of all the other residents and heard someone yell, "Fire!" I looked over and saw the huge blaze that had broken out in the adjacent house, a little too close for comfort. I shook my head, "This looks really bad," I said, and it was rightly evident, but the truth I kept was that the blaze was also an incredible sight, so close, hot, and high, with colorful flames reaching up and overtaking the building's entire facade. Hope no one's getting burned in there, I thought to myself. It was just yesterday that the firemen had been called out to our residence, but here they came again, followed by the same contingent of police, to attempt another successful rescue. Soon the firemen attacked and raised their hoses to douse out the flames. Between the freaking woman locking herself in a car the day before, and the sudden fire, things were getting exciting around the Ranch. I asked around, "Do you know how the fire started?" Everyone—ops, residents, firemen and firewomen—shook their heads, disbelief drooping their faces as all stared into the smoke, all that was left of the flames. No one had any clue how it began, and no one offered a response. One guy I knew from the neighboring house, Glen, was still unaccounted for as the firemen persisted to fight the fire's core. The gang of them hoisted their ladder up to the second floor, and none of them stepped through the window he had just broken to check on the poor missing guy, and if it was still possible, I supposed, to rescue him. Another fireman climbed the ladder to the second floor and there appeared Glen, streaked with soot, being ushered by a fireman down the ladder and to the ground. He was coughing but turned out to be okay. One girl's mother came running in from somewhere and took her daughter in her arms. I had no idea whether she had been in the house or was just scared by the fire. In any case, the people were definitely out of danger. "Oh my God," one woman wrapped in a blanket said. "We won't have a place to live now." "I've lost all of my things," another person said. We all stared at the spouts of water putting out the blaze and causing a spinning cloud of smoldering smoke. That evening, all of us residents, patients, clients, and various of our acquaintances were either sitting around gossiping about the cause of the fire—who, if anyone we knew, set it—or requesting to go to the hospital to get our skin and lungs checked out. "The cause of the fire was a cigarette left on a couch," Tony, who can be a bit of a "know-it-all," proclaimed. I didn't think so because no smoking is allowed inside the residences, and we always are monitored. Lucky for me, I'm a non-smoker, though I chew tobacco almost every night. But as far as I know, chewing tobacco isn't flammable. "Tony c'mon," I said. "It must have been a grease fire." I went to bed without a guilty conscience. Some of the displaced from the adjacent residence went to bed down in shelters. One person, to my mind, from across the way had to be the arsonist. The following morning delivered a bright red sky, and from the way I understand the weather, this indicates a trying day to come. The displaced residents started to come back in a small droves from the shelter with no place to go but to double up in our residence. Over the next few days, Spring Lake Ranch was overrun with insurance adjusters inspecting the house, surveying the damage, although there wasn't much to inspect or survey what with the house's burned to-a-crisp empty shell. The displaced were also given new clothing, telephones, and food. We all seemed to be empathetic for those affected by the fire, but a lot of what they lost couldn't be replaced. All of us residents continued our banter about who possibly could have started the fire, what to do about it, what went wrong, but we never heard or figured out how it actually started, or who the arsonist was. The point was that there wouldn't be any neighboring house for a while, and that would make things different around Spring Lake Ranch. The administrators will have to rebuild the destroyed second dwelling with the insurance they'll receive. It shouldn't be too arduous on their wallet. Years later, the rumor still persisted that a burning cigarette left on the house's living-room couch had sparked the blaze. I can believe that. I am also a nicotine fanatic like all these incendiary people, but at least I chew rather than light up to get my fix.

* * *

The first weekend of the New Year has arrived. I was making plans for many events when Eileen called me. "Hello, Jamie, I really miss you," she said. "Oh yeah? Do you want to see a movie?" I asked. "Sure. I really want to see One Flew Over the Cuckoo's Nest. "People in our residence love that movie, including myself. Can you blame us? Cartoon characters can be like a version of us, if one uses their imagination, but far worse or are we? "Eileen Will we go on to plan a lot of events?" Eileen and I, to keep our relationship solid, and our minds, bodies, and souls together. We are very much in love, or at least it feels that way, even at this early stage. I still don't officially consider her my girlfriend for life. But she's becoming downcast.

I am being real but I don't believe that Eileen ever loved me much I just bought the lie out of the believing we were going together and had a future together. The hype settled down concerning the recent bad luck—the screaming intruder, then the burned-out property next door. Mobile homes were set up around the Ranch to house the displaced. The area took on the appearance of a Formula I race, with all the mobile homes, containers, and cars and vans everywhere. The grassy front yard became matted with footsteps and a bit muddy and there were tire marks of all kinds from the local dignitaries still driving in and out over the incident. We all ate in one house, and the three mobile homes were now occupied by eight residents. That's a crowd. As the winter progressed, the weather turned to snow. One day I teamed up with Glen, who had decided to stay rather than go to a shelter after the fire in his residence, to catch a bus and head out somewhere, starting from the major road that runs east to west and parallel to the front of the Ranch property at the base of a hill. My new cohort wanted the head due east to run an errand, and I could just as easily gone that direction, too, but I got distracted about which destination I wanted to head, so I stopped dead in my tracks in the cold and waited for a bus going in the opposite direction—but never took the bus anywhere because it was too cold. And the truth was, even though I had gone to the road with my "buddy" and all, I didn't care to travel with him. Why? Because he had once stolen $40 from me, and when I confronted him over it he only gave me $20 back. After many mornings of sleeping late, this past Sunday, still early in the New Year, I was up at the very earliest sliver of dawn, and saw the ground covered in snow. Both two-story houses, including the sad skeleton of the torched one, now stood amid a winter wonderland. For fun during the year I am planning to collect photos of football games and hopefully sell them in a flea market at the local church charity auctions. I also got back to making my Plaster of Paris molds into sculptures. It will take time and patience to sell my artworks at the church. It's easy to sit there staring at your work in front of you and wait for some magic to sell your work for you, but it doesn't work that way. I need steady, more reliable and lucrative employment. Some very cold air rushed in on this holiday celebrating Dr. Martin Luther King, Jr., which happens to be today. The news claimed it was 28 degrees Fahrenheit. I don't mind the cold, I like walking in the snow, and I skied a lot as a youngster. I had no problem walking around in the frigid environment, even across long distances, to run some errands. I wanted to pick up soap for the washing machine, soda, and some postage stamps from the post office. A lot of the hobbies I keep these days, the aquarium, the molded sculptures, the photographs, I kept as a young boy as part of a curriculum. I guess I retained the skills to still do them well? I swell with pride at the memory of the 1st Prize I received from the Greenwich Environmental Council for a photograph I took of a man working on a roof with a blinding lamp in the foreground. I had learned how to develop prints in a darkroom in high school. I can still take wonderful pictures. If I had my way, I'd like to be the next Ansel Adams. The town's snow shoveling was up again and in force. Another incident at the group home that left me sullen and quiet across the MLK holiday occurred late at night: some medication had gone missing. The staff came around to wake all of us up, and the three of us in our room were put into miserable moods, all because of their stupid staff paranoia. They (house staff) searched the entire house with a fine-toothed comb but found nothing. To my left, as I ran downstairs the woman whose meds were stolen was trying to figure out what she had to do to find the thief or replace her meds. Due to the paranoid atmosphere, I wasn't convinced anyone had even stolen them. Maybe she misplaced it or took the wrong dosage, anything was possible with certain of the residents. Behind me on a couch in the sitting room, a girl kept complaining, "Why can't we all get along?" I guess she was feeling paranoid or she had issues with socialization. Her comment seemed entirely appropriate to the holiday. That night, after the frantic scene had calmed and the paranoid heat blew over—no overdoses under duress means all good—and things seemed to be getting back to normal, we all sat and watched the movie of that night, The Bourne Legacy. I found that film to be action packed but lacking in depth. What else the hell did I expect? During the film, I had the thought that the reasons for all the pseudo-abhorrent feelings in the group residence I call home were not the natural feelings of the residents, but the feelings caused by all the medications we take. It's like med on med, as our doctors never hesitate to write prescriptions for our so-called health. Me? My docs prescribe me mood enhancers. Prozac is one such mood enhancing medication, and I take it. Clozaril is an antidepressant, and I also take it. Both these medications keep me feeling satisfactory. The same doctors that give us all these meds all seem to favor Freudian psychotherapy, which to me is just that. I assume most doctors are monetarily oriented, anyhow. At least we are all stuck here next to one another so we can air and listen to all our grievances. We can even scream to all of mankind if we choose to. The road toward mental illness recovery is a tough one. I give my best strong entity during therapy. After many years of it, one realizes that a psychiatric doctor is really different from a mentor. Many of us come out of hospitals in mortified states, while others just seem to come out simply tolerating their existences. When I come out of the psych hospital, I always feel rejuvenated, but also highly unsatisfied, like the entire stay was just a means to an end. Is that what this time was all about? Letters from which veer the attending doctor who attended to me about my most recent visit always manage to reach my resident counselor:

Dear Dr. Shatterhand,

Jamie stopped by EPIH today to pay me a visit. I had been his psychiatrist before he moved to the CR in Spring Lake Ranch. He seemed to be doing well on the Clozaril— thinking clearly and keeping organized, but during our visit he seemed markedly downcast and depressed compared to his usual state as I remember it. Subjectively, too, he experiences low energy and depressive thoughts. Would you discuss with him the question of antidepressant medicine? Possibly change one drug or a change of dosage. In any case, please call me.

Dr. Pott

Downcast and depressed. Can you frigging blame me? To me, this was a letter suggesting I switch doctors, not medications or dosages. Because I do much better working with healthy people as opposed to programs that involve mental health "consumers" (as we are so often referred to) or ex-patients who persist in their depressed states of finance or mind or whatever. I had my times with no money, living on Social Security is an economic fare worse than death. But I had my super British step-mom to mentor me along. A doctor with his social workers alone wouldn't have brought me along. There are at any one time about fifteen people in the Ranch community, so we do not see everyone around, nor know who is coming and who is going all the time, because it can be a fast turn round, and that doesn't do a lot for a person's sense of trust or stability. Glen has a visible scar due to a car accident. It is a jagged rip along his left cheek about three inches long. The scar has ruined my self-esteem vision of him to the cusp of danger, so I had to watch him suspiciously. I also has a visible scar, some minor bump on the forehead near his hairline. The bump had made a self-conscious (at one time), Jamie could relate but never get close., Harry Potter in the series also visualized this in a portrayal diagnosis. I just received his scar from a skiing accident at Mt Washington in the White mountains…Not even considering this I did not accept Glen's offer of Klonopin. In my state of mind, it would have been more dangerous than ever. In the mental health arena, foul play can occur. Weeks later, after the Harry Potter movie and the Bourne Legacy, I tried to write in my journal while lying in bed but the music downstairs, some monotonous thumping DJ music, was getting too loud. The consumers downstairs were either still watching TV, doing their evening chores, or smoking outside, the same activities they do every night. "It's too loud," I yelled at whoever the culprit was. "Turn that crap down!" It was Glen who yelled back, "Sorry about that! Just trying to re-energize myself." Glen's "music" was making me too nervous to keep sane. It is common that for most people music invigorates the soul and gets one up and doing activity. The next day, a Sunday, the house finally became peaceful and more sullen again, especially after the fire, the screaming woman, and now the missing medication incidents. The afternoon was arriving in splendid form. It was a cool breezy afternoon with a clear and cloudless sky. My chore of the day was cleaning the residence van, which the staff often uses for the Ranch's shopping runs. Clients, if they can afford them, are allowed to own cars. One reason I want to make more money is to get a nice car like a good American sedan or a fine Volkswagen, and, of course, to afford to pay for the insurance. I just realized if I lived alone and didn't have the community pressure, I'd probably lapse in my house rent. Houses with humans in them get dirty very fast, so I'd probably live with others /alone in an ever-dirty house. I still want my own place someday, though. I'll take that risk to have more space for myself. The following

Saturday after that last splendid Sunday, jury duty called in the form of a letter. Somehow, this particular letter excited me. Why? Because I knew I wouldn't have to go! I enthusiastically filled out the return questionnaire. Also why? Because I had heard that the son of a lawyer or a psychologically troubled person could never perform jury duty, though I also heard the authorities eased this rule. In any event, I was out to go on both counts, but still reconsidered the things I thought I knew and decided to contact the jury people, sending along a note from my psychiatrist to tell them why I should be excused from jury duty, thrilled goosely by the good chance I wouldn't have to go.

Eureka

I don't know what tomorrow holds, but on the weekend my housemate George and I walked a mile to spend a Sunday morning at Mass, as I have a lot to pray about. Namely, better mental and financial health. While I prayed, the preacher gave us wine and bread. I'm not supposed to drink alcohol, I am incorrigible with booze, but one sip of wine couldn't hurt. Jesus drank wine, right? The preacher's sermon concerned "Humbleness." How we ought to learn to love ourselves first, and then try to again become proud, humble, and good Americans. I offered my best prayers for the weeks ahead, praying for more self-esteem and empowerment.

Why can't I be independent? I asked the man upstairs. The answer to my prayer rebounded from somewhere right back into my head: Because what employer would put up with your inexperience, Jamie? Sitting in the pew, I went over my schedule. Next Monday, I'll go to the library to read. Tuesday it'll be more therapy and another visit to the doctor. I am not looking forward to going to the doctor for another checkup. They'll take more blood to monitor my meds, and it will make me dizzy when I stand up too quickly afterward, which I always do. Who looks forward to getting dizzy? Sitting at Mass on

Sunday with other Christians really lifted up my mood and spirit, but by Wednesday, I'm down in the dumps again, drooping in a bit of a hound dog attitude. I get that way for a while sometimes, but somehow I manage to pick up and continue on toward the day's challenges. The meds seem to basically tire me out. I have no anger line down my forehead or temple I am only a "Peter Pan" advice kind of fellow, I have to catch that second wind to really keep me going strong. I awoke late and applied for a photo job, almost doing nothing but waiting to hear back the entire rest of the day. Thursday I was watching The Last Picture Show, a black and white classic film, with Tony when the phone rang. "Tony, could you answer it, please?" I asked. "Nah. I'm too tired," he responded. He continued to gawk at Candice Bergen in the movie. Jamie never answered either because Jamie was avoiding the pay phone since he now has a cell. The truth is I think Tony doesn't like to answer phone calls because he never gets any. The telephone rang and rang until Jamal finally ran downstairs, probably out of frustration, to answer it. "Hello?" Jamal said. "Mom, hey…" I've come to the conclusion that my situation here sucks. I have limited freedom, no car, and no privacy. I have to constantly check-in and be driven everywhere. As Tony stares at the movie and Jamal continues to listen to his mom, I remember the time my certified social worker drove me to a day treatment center, which housed a program for us consumers of mental illness, I say to Tony, "We had gone in to the painted building and waited in the reception area. I took a tour of the center and the grounds, and Tony, guess what I did?" "What?" "I refused to sign in to be forced to spend days there and told them I would like to dis-enroll from my present program as soon as possible." "Wow." Tony didn't seem too impressed, but that didn't surprise me because is he ever? The point is all these social workers and psych systems seem to do is keep shoving psych rehab programs in our faces wherever they happen to appear, at group meetings, doctor appointments, patient socializations, even at the café. That week, I decided to rethink my current itinerary. I talked to my dad and he suggested I get a job. Really original, Dad, I thought to myself. He has good intentions, but jobs are scarce around here. I was planning to donate blood like they advertise at the local school on Friday, but because I still had meds in my system, I decided not to. I don't think that our systems with so many meds inside would at all affect giving pints of blood away to someone who really needed them. Instead, I spent the next free days riding the local buses to my various appointments. The thing I re-learned that day is that my spending has to be curtailed. I have to stop spending. Thank God I don't have the same horrible smoking habit everyone else seems to have—that would really burn up my money in addition to all the necessities. When I got home later, "How's it going, Jamie?" Jamal asked. "Fine," I said. "Thanks for asking. You?" "I'm having leftover ravioli," Jamal said. "My mother is in Florida," he for some reason told Tony and me. Two of us, George, another resident, and I were conspiring to go on a shopping spree. When we did, we bought bicycles and wall paintings. After I finished up in the last store, where I had bought a few tins of chewing tobacco, as we walked back up the hill from the stores toward the community residence, we were quiet. As we were walking and starting to converse, I had been playing around with numbers in my head as I chewed some gum I had bought during our spree. We stopped by a roadside convenience store to pick up some lottery tickets like "Numbers" and "Win 4." It was only Monday and when I got back, my roommate Jamal and I decided and watch Monday Night Football on television. The week before, I had retained an employment test in and around my free days—spent shopping or hobbies, usually—so I could try to get a job with the Census Bureau. I took the exam three times and scored in the high 70s each time. Not too shabby, but shabby enough not to be considered for hire. After watching football, we watched some soap reruns. One thing that stood out to me was when the overly made-up actor said to his mother, "I'll wait until you come to your senses." If you even barely listen, you can get a lot of Peter Pan advice from TV soaps, but it doesn't sink into your brain and seldom pays off in actual life. I rarely watch soaps, but for some reason I did that night. It wasn't a lesson to me, because when I was in a hospital institution all we had was television and medication. Both sedated. Come to my senses, now! I still feel too dependent on my father. I want to be a braver, stronger person, only beholden to myself. Perhaps this was because my father was a Taurus, and bull-headed to match, and I was—am—the youngest of the family, so I always felt like I lagged behind and still struggled to keep up. For me, the most sensible way to react is to work. Look at it like this: Dad would say "possession is 90% of the law." He had the power of Attorney, the big house, the wealth etc. That's 90% of power over our family. What do I have when introduced into adulthood, but an attitude that holds promise for 90%. Holds promise No guarantees. I just keep up with my brother, as competition leads to a win Or at least second-string efforts. The Spring Lake Ranch house sometimes is completely unable to hold it together. We are all pulled in different directions with the diversity we have, which some want to embrace and others abhor. As far as the direction I am pulled, I just don't like being there at the residence much, especially during the day. That's why I always end up riding the buses around. I'd really prefer to have a reason to go to an office and just think or express my thoughts on paper. I could easily focus on one type of employment, especially as it would give me an office to escape into. It's just that no one will give me the chance to work. At least I've told myself no one will. Around Spring Lake Ranch if there's no chores, besides sleep, watching TV is the biggest event, especially either Monday Night Football or the Saturday afternoon basketball games with college or pro teams. But I'd rather make sculptures or paintings than glue my eyes to televised sports. If I had to engage in sport, I'd rather shoot baskets than watch someone else do it (much better) on TV. If I do choose to watch television, it's usually Sunday night television, intellectual political discussions like the Chris Mathew's Show, for one example. The latest art news in my life is that a couple of my paintings, of water lilies, have been included in the college alumni art organization show, and I am working on a new sculpture of a human head—a bloke. This most recent Sunday, I dropped by the counselors' office to do something unique compared to the other two to three times per day I find myself there. I had a discussion about my three-month expenses with one counselor in particular, Rosemary. As we talked, my eyes glanced down to a notebook on the desk and saw some program notes—about me! They said: "Jamie, you are doing very well. You are meeting your goals. By next winter you will be able to move. Jamie seems to isolate from people." And? I thought. "When I finally got back to my room" "I can get along with everybody if I want to try.", Tony felt the need to tell me, "You left the bathtub full of water." "Oh yeah?" I said, as if it was a surprise, though I suddenly realized I had indeed forgotten. "Sorry about that, Tony." "It's all right, the tub was half empty, anyway." Tony said. Kinda like Tony himself, I thought. Sometimes I'm surprised the three of us can share the same room together because we even have a hard time listening to one another, and an even harder time "getting" along with one another. I guess it's a good thing for our three-way friendship that Jamal watches too much TV, talks to his mother too much, and religiously attends his mental health program, and that Tony sleeps a lot, steadily works, or would rather listen to music than talk. Their activities always leave me time to do my own thing, "isolate" myself, as was written about me. There might be some reasons for our differences. These guys never had the great upbringing I had, which enabled me tremendously. I had an early childhood illness: mumps meningitis. Am I feeling sorry for them? They might have had wonderful childhoods, for all I know. So what is our common problem? It was the next Sunday that I awoke around 7 a.m. to Jamal sleeping in late. After I shopped for coffee at the convenience store, I reunited with him back in the room. "Jamal, good morning," I said. "Huh? Morning, Jamie, I am going to get some more sleep," Jamal said. He hadn't changed his bed sheets in a while. I couldn't believe he had just gotten up and now wanted to go back to sleep already. It wasn't like him. It puzzles me how I could be toward others in certain cases, but is pathetic how mental patients conduct our emotions and how we feel and the way we act. It doesn't always make sense to "out ideas." We look out after ourselves first. Then a gander at the others. After a minute of staring at dozing Jamal, he finally popped his eyes open, got up and announced, "I'm going to take a shower." "Sounds like a plan for the day, Jamal. Finally." I had plans for the weekend, and that Sunday morning was already bright and sunny. Tony and I went to the coffee shop, and he called his girl Dawn over to pick him up from the Ranch. Tony actually up and doing some activity on a Sunday when he was not forced to work, when he usually did nothing or slept in, totally surprised me. As far as Jamal and his external relations, I have never seen him with a girlfriend, and by that I mean a lover. I am just glad to have Eileen as a semi-girlfriend. Once, I told Jamal in confidence when Tony wasn't around, "Jamal, you are a nice guy." "Jamie, you're a nice guy, too." Nice guys don't necessarily always finish last. Jamal headed downstairs to get dinner ready. He was planning to make a chef's salad. Soon he called up, "Dinner's ready!" I said, "I am not having any dinner, thank you. Chef's salad is not my thing." I heard someone running up the stairs. Jamal appeared in the room, "No, no, no, no dinner?" he said. I eventually went down to the dining room to eat. At dinner, we spoke the usual rhetoric about wanting a smoke, how tired we were, and rock and roll lyrics. It would be so redundant for the future of

America if rock – and-roll was all there was remaining on the scene. I mean, in other countries they have various musical forms and venues. Our Top of the Pops are the same old sounds. At least on radio broadcasts. It was with this animosity stirring me up that I spoke up to Jamal. "Another thing, Jamal, you should buy some toilet paper for us. I have been supplying almost all of it lately," I said. "I don't buy it because I supply my own," Jamal replied. The next day, the three of us were driven up to the local polling place to vote in the general election. We went in and talked to the polling people. A man asked for our names before we went into the booth to vote. When he got to me, Tony chimed in, "He'll be a college graduate, but now he works in a gas station." Tony's true comment irked me at first, but it was also refreshing since I am indeed headed for a degree. He wasn't trying to make me feel obscure or belittled in any way, but his ribbing humor brought the lows up and people love to be pleased and complemented at the same time. Or at least I do. He was being pessimistic! As much as Tony can irritate me crazy, he can also really lift my spirits. One main reason is because he dresses like a relic from a long-past age. This particular day he was dressed in torn blue jeans and a Megadeth rock t-shirt. Come on now, Tony, that '60s era is basically over, try to finally dress for success, I muttered to myself. Jamal had his turn at voting and commented, "Now my vote can, can, can be counted, too." After we voted, I said to Tony, "My plan is to work more so I can get a place of my own." "Oh, yeah." "Yeah. I am predicting I will never poll at this place again." Since I became an adult, I've had to move polling places every few years. I just can't put up with this habit that the staff has to shuttle us around for something so simple like going to vote. It's our freedom, not their control. The reason I switched voting places all the time was because I moved around a lot and lived in a lot of areas. We left the polling place after the three of us had voted and were driven back to the community residence. Tony remained outside to have a smoke. The psycho/social return to normal living takes time with many different facets. We have to figure it out for ourselves, But certainly the house counselors help. In my case my stepmother was the biggest catalyst to help. Me and Jamal went back to our room and lied down, staring at the ceiling. "We voted, Jamal," I said. "Can you believe it?" "Yes, we did and no I can't," he concluded. As I did a little gardening the next day, weeding and watering, I decided I couldn't agree more with how I voted. With doing the optimum he can be, and feeling in backwaters, going up the staircase which can be done easily inside or something. Only I conscientiously would take the steps only up because the scenario is here and it will stay here And any dream of making it big someday is my gnawing aspiration. Jamal could believe it! I didn't lie to him To Tony and Eileen, I am not so convincing.

A New Job

When my new job as a service station gasoline attendant started a new beginning was at yonder and I was encroaching my dignity with a grateful, thankful heart. I generally came home at 6:30 p.m. and the guys would always save me some dinner. Tony asked, as always, "How was work?" "Fine," I always replied. "Wow, such a handsome lad now," Jamal proclaimed, referring to a photograph of me he had seen at the station. Both he and Tony, and even me, I suppose, had made that picture into the running joke of our shared room. While I've been working, Jamal has still been watching a lot of television. However, I've been noticing he doesn't watch as long as before. Why? He has no real other hobby.

He just flips through the channels and lies on his bed with his hand cupped over his mouth, for what reason, I don't know. The room is quiet. I can hear the fish aquarium bubbling next to my bed. Watching those fish being fed today? If Jamal walks in the room and turns his television on and off once more, I am going to curse him out, something I would not love to do, and did. "Dammit, Jamal! In front of the boobtube box again?" I shouldn't be such a cynical critic. A year has passed since I wrote these notes: on a sunny day, sitting on the verandah, I received a telephone call late one weekday morning from a fellow in a gasoline service station asking me if I would like to work at his service station. That's what got the job ball rolling, that "cooking with gas" I mentioned. Almost literally. After the call, I rode my bicycle eight miles for the interview, and they hired me on the spot. I had a job. I am really kinda happy to be making some real money, I repeated to myself and almost couldn't stop. I got so excited that maybe now I'd be able to get a car and have my own place. Now I have been at the job for one full year and never missed a day. I am gaining growth through no impling but rather implementing. I am getting independent. They have a nice black Lab dog there by the name of Casey. I show up on time and most importantly to me, I produce something. I pump gasoline. I do have some problems at work. A lot of wishy-washy stuff goes through my mind and I catch myself talking about changing jobs, when I know I probably shouldn't, not yet. Sarcasm at work, so I thought, can go a long way toward helping any relationship (with a boss) but I am usually met with cheerless and thankless sentiments. You see, I have highs and lows and doing the job— any job—requires a constant reality check due to so many years of unemployment and therapy. No relationship with a boss is anything to ponder over. My boss is Jason. Once he gave me a nostalgia popcorn maker and because I knew his old man was a city policeman and a colonel in the U.S. Army, my response was, "I got my popcorn from the kernel." I thought my line was funny, but nobody else at the station seemed to, especially Jason. A credit card machine clings to the station wall and sometimes I swipe the credit cards and sometimes I collect the cash. I prefer to collect the cash. It's more direct. Sometimes the credit-card machine gets tied-up and says: WAITING FOR LINE. It can get this way for long-distance calls, as well. Some ladies sit idling in their cars doing some paperwork, and I return their cards as soon as possible. I often joke with customers waiting on the tied-up credit card machine. I tell them this is my new bread-and-butter and I am "butter" off for it. Another of my word jokes. No one laughs. A car came in from outside the USA and I gassed it up. I asked the driver, "How are you?" but he didn't speak any English, so I motioned. He gave the fee, which I was grateful for. Sometimes I let myself get to the verge of quitting, which I know is stupid of me. I'll get so sick of work or Jason will get so sick of me threatening to quit that I'll have to quit, or get fired. My daily cash-outs are getting good, I just need to renew my attitude and stick it out every day and watch my irony. I can see now how my mental ill attitude equates to my getting sick and tired of working. One problem it is really difficult for me to be reliable because I want to attend to other more important matters. With the work I do, I do okay. I keep persevering and I get the job done. Once I was waiting on the gas pump island for the next car to pull up, and on the way down to take the customer, I missed the step-down and I fell on my hands and knees. It smarted but I brushed myself off and quickly stepped back up. I hoped Jason didn't notice what a klutz (spatz) I am. One year into the job, the job seems to be getting easier. I think I'll last, even get along with everyone here. Maybe. One night, Billy, Jason's father, had me pondering a question. "Anything look different around here, Jim?" he asked. I hardly understand my boss sometimes, let alone his pointed questions. I looked around and then up at the neon sign, which was glowing a bright red, white, and blue. "It is called Gas' n' Go," Billy said. That's what he meant about something being "different" around the station. I hadn't noticed that they put up a new neon sign. One day on the job, I ran into one of our mechanics Ed, cursing out Jason about his temper. The guy had been covering for me while I emptied the used oil in the ground storage. "Hey! Make sure that's the right container hole for the used oil!" Jason had screamed, then turned to scream at me. "Dammit, Jim he'll put that oil in the wrong place." Ed said to Jason. I was completely confident. This gave me the chance to vent my own true feelings. "I am very inexperienced but I know that the oil goes in here, so, I've already proved myself to be a worthy helper and justified my work," I said, before getting into my other routines. "Real fights and a fist in the nose could have hurt much more than this screwed-up, lousy, place," Ed said. "You, Jim, are forced to work. Jason is not forced to work." No fights occurred at the station that day, but I was starting to loathe the place. I was the last out at five to 6, when I saw a man walking into the garage. "Are you here for your car?" "Yes, I called before. I told whoever answered I'd be here shortly before six," the man said. "Fair enough. I'll wait for you. Your keys are in the car. You can pay us tomorrow," I said, and then waited for him to back out in his car. My good deed for the day, letting the guy pay another time. That's called "developing customer trust." After the man drove off, the rest of us who remained at the station joked around a bit, or at least the other guys did. I'm usually the serious one. Jason and Jay, a mechanic, reached over and touched a button on my shirt with his fingers, and when I looked down, they tried to flick my nose. Actually, Jay took his finger and snubbed my nose. I wanted to do it back to him, but I'm too mellow for that. I have a new nickname here: "Spanky." Why, I don't know. Normal? I accepted a nickname with my face still shining towards the sun everyday. Jason had left the shop at 11 a.m. one day and had taken his motorcycle to another state to buy 500 dollars worth of lottery tickets. He came back around 3:30 p.m. At least he witnessed that both I and my customers were in good spirits. Was I doing a good service for Jason and Billy, I wondered? The truth is, it's not a bad job. And I stood up for myself to this boss Jason. Sometimes the weather is too awful to stand outside all day by the pumps, but the pay is all right. Whenever I go back home, I'm always hopeful to maintain a positive attitude. Finally, I reached the end of another work week. It's Friday and of course, Friday is payday and therefore the best day of the week. Sometimes after payday, I go to the local pub's "Happy Hour" and talk to local laborers and secretaries about the day, or we tell each other jokes, or just drink beer. This pub has a superb buffet and it's free so it makes it even more superb. I am being careful about bars. Sometimes at the end of the week, I go to Hartford, my usual retreat from Spring Lake Ranch and all its mental health rhetoric and too-familiar surroundings. There is a clubhouse in Hartford I spend time in: the Chrysalis Center. The telephone in our residence's foyer rang and there was a short message for me from Eileen: "Oh Jamie, I forgot to tell you about taking your medication with you when we travel." I called her back and left a message of my own: "Eileen! Oh! So we are still enforcing that Good! I want to see you tomorrow. Want to come to Hartford? Call me." Over the next week, Tony, Jamal and I had a few disagreements at night when I got home from the station. Tony asked, "Do you feed the station's dog for pay too, or just pump gas?" I tried to sound important, "Well, the boss pays me for doing the service and I do errands for him, I feed the dog as goodwill." For some reason, Tony became irate, "Stop the mumbo jumbo, Jamie!" When he's irate, Tony only accepts straight answers. "I feed the dog as goodwill".

Christmas Time

It is December, the end of the year and close to Christmas, and I'm at the station. "Hello," I said into my cell phone. "Hi Jamie, how are you doing?" Eileen asked. "Doing well," I said. After she left me a message on the residence phone, I'd left a message on her voicemail that I'd be in her neck of the woods getting my teeth looked at by a dentist. She never got back to me. "Did you get me diamonds yet?" she inquired. I chuckled, which really upset her. "Working on it," I retorted. I knew making a joke around the holidays was in poor taste, but I did anyway. "Diamonds are only a girl's best friend." "How was your day?" she asked. I didn't say much more because work had fully exhausted me. "Well, let's see. My brother Harold gave me an early Christmas present," I told her. "A barometer." "Oh yeah??" Eileen asked. "Yup." I stand on my feet all day, running from the garage to the pumps and back again, I have to make some sort of conversation, right? So this gadget, the barometer, made the perfect conversation piece for that, as well as generally passing the time. Now I could always tell the temperature and the weather, so the gift was a real help and nice surprise. "I'm tired," I said. "What day are we going to that Astoria restaurant?" We had planned to dine with her folks sometime over Christmas, which I hate because her mother is such an overzealous mom. I mean she babysits her daughter so much that I feel the repercussions on the other side, my end with all my ill-emotional climbing on my Dad's emotions and successes. "Christmas Eve," she replied. "I'm really looking forward to that," I lied. "That's next Monday," she went on to say. Which made me think I need to go shopping. Next weekend is practically Christmas already. "You could stay Christmas Eve if you like," she told me. "Give me a call again towards the end of the week and we'll figure it out." "Okay, babe." The biggest snowstorm of the year soon blanketed everything with about a foot of light powdery fluffy stuff. My Christmas hope was that I would find an agency that will find me an apartment I can afford. A lot of the apartments I am hoping for are close to the shopping area and the service station. Not one agency has got back to me yet. I am getting geared up to see Eileen, who has decided to have a party, complete with guests. I went to the station and I put gas into my first new car, a dodge dart, planning to pay at a later day, and I fed Casey, the owners' Lab. Then I drove to Springfield to take a swim at the YMCA. The Y has a pool as part of their gym. The cost is six dollars. I paid the fee, changed into my swim trunks and swam about a quarter of a mile. A quarter of a mile is eight laps. It was all unhindered strokes, and no one is around because it's a Saturday. After the swim, I drove my vehicle over to the strip of stores in Springfield and shopped there to buy a woman's scarf for Eileen for Christmas. First I looked in the Dress Barn, a mom-and-pop store, because Eileen told me to shop there. I like to shop there because they are struggling with competition from the big stores and, basically, shopping at these kinds of places keeps the local stores in business. Eileen wants a $100-gift certificate for Christmas but with the economic recession, she won't get it, and certainly not diamonds. I don't have that kind of money! Not yet. I got to Eileen's house early for her Christmas party. She had cooked a turkey and had the table all set up for a buffet. Slowly, people trickled in: Rosemary and Mark arrived, then Dave, then Dave's roommate, Mr. Mines, who was invited at the last minute (it was I who called him to come over). These were mostly Eileen's friends but I knew Dave and Mr. Mines. Liz called and said she was too beat to show up. Eileen's house is a two-story job. The stairs start in the middle of the house on the first floor, flanked by a living room, dining room, and kitchen, which form a sort of perimeter. I put everyone's coats upstairs in Eileen's bedroom. Everybody behaved themselves, thankfully. As soon as most of the guests had gathered, I surprised Eileen with the gift: the scarf, with a nice design on it. She said it was wonderful. She thanked me and we hugged. After that, none of us wasted any time, we all sat down to eat our turkey dinner. Then we took our cigarette breaks, at least the others stepped outside for one or too many. After we stuffed ourselves into a stupor, we all went into Eileen's living room to watch a film version of the seasonal favorite, A Christmas Story. It was hard to make any real conversation during the film, but I realized most of these people came from rehabilitation centers so who says they are really my friends? It was Eileen's idea to invite them, so I had just played along so she could have some guests over around the holiday. For some reason, Mr. Mines, Mark, and Rosemary decided to leave in the middle of A Christmas Story, during the scene where the lead boy gets a fist in the face. Mr. Mines walked over to the stairs. "Could I have my coat?" he asked. "Yeah, sure," I replied, and got off the couch and ran up the stairs into Eileen's bedroom to get his coat for him. As he was putting his coat on, we talked about the rehabilitation centers, about jobs, careers, and how we intended to employ ourselves. The other guests, I knew, were just happy to exist on Social Security and had no interest in talking about getting real jobs. It was evident that no one was really there to even watch the movie, just there for the feast.

* * *

Eileen and I received permission to lodge at the family co-op in Fayston on Christmas Eve. That night we stopped at both her parents and mine. Helen and Dad gave us lots of presents: clothes, books, and toys (well, little joke ones). The weather was cold but clear and we made a fire in the fireplace. It sparkled and illuminated me as I sat next to the hearth in a big easy chair. I wish Eileen and I would have had as nice an affair, but a bunch of virtual strangers lying around over turkey and A Christmas Story? Why she and I remained so uninspired during the holiday, we will never understand. Both Dad and Helen told me I seemed much more focused, even that I was a pleasant person to be around now. It was Helen who helped with her practice acting of throwing ill-emotions right back at me. I'd made progress, it's true, what with writing, working a job, and a potentially blossoming fine relationship with Eileen. Could be worse. My past behavior had been much fickler. Most people only have a handful of good friends in life, and even those might just be acquaintances. Come to Christmas Day in Greenwich, Helen found me and said, "Your father gets in these awful moods." Later, Dad turned the question around toward me, "Do you remember when you'd get so moody with your mother?" What's with all the talk of the family moods? I thought. I didn't know the answer. "I don't know," I said. "Isn't it me who's in the most awful moods all back in my teenage years?" I'm going to make a New Year's resolution to try to be more cheerful in life, love, and laughter. And I'm going to try to see my moods as two-way streets. As a Christmas gift, I gave Dad a painting I'd done, an actual finished piece. It was a scene of the 18th Hole at some famous golf course I painted by numbers. "Your dad loves golf, now he'll be really exuberant, for a while at least," Helen said. Better than not being exuberant, I thought. Christmas had been a truly wonderful time. I was so elated to be a part of a super Christmas affair with my family on that 25th of December, and thinking back, Eileen's family gathering hadn't been so bad either.

The Co-op

At the start of the New Year, 2020, I said to myself, I have a place to live, I have a job, and I have a girlfriend. Also, I have a place to vacation and another car. The "new" car is a used Hyundai Elantra as I put the dodge Dart up on blocks to store away. I can honestly say I have most of the normal amenities that everyone who has a modicum of a life has. The gnawing idea of wanting to be rich, and right now. I am a financially exclusive person, but in reality I am a pauper. Hey, not everyone reaches the highest grade. I dont sweat it anymore. Have I missed the boat of marrying and raising a family? Maybe. My brother and sister can cover for me. I am single and middle aged but it feels just alright. There is so much out there in the real world, one just has to look and explore. Getting the first step out of the family nest is synonymous with the longest journey starts with the first step In more revelations about God's love it can be very difficult leading this life but He assures us He is with me every step of the way. My New Year's resolutions, and on New Year's Eve, Eileen and I went to "First Night" Hartford to see a few bands perform. We went to a sea chantey performance on a date where I knew the musician singing the chanteys. I walked in the place with Eileen just as he finished a song. "Yes,

David!!" we shouted, and clapped our hands. We really enjoyed his songs, yes! Next we went to the town common and rode the Ferris wheel. I know Hartford very well, but much to my surprise, after riding the Ferris wheel, I was so dizzy I thought I was exiting out onto the street side, but ended up, with Eileen in tow, exiting onto the river side. It was all new because I hadn't been there in years. No more Ferris wheeling for me. We stopped for a coffee and I spilled my cup and Eileen and I didn't clean it up, we just left. We stayed around Hartford until the clock struck midnight, then we welcomed 2020 with a glance at the fireworks. The fireworks blasted right in front of us in the town center and that's where we had parked the Hyundai. I entered 2020 in a very special state of mind. It was a Sunday in January and everyone was watching the original Batman in our room. I hadn't seen the program since the 1960s during its first season on prime time tv Until then I hadn't realized just how nutty the show had been with all its cheesy costumes I sat on the edge of my bed and laughed at the batman and joked: its a Halloween episode. I folded my comforter and it read God loves you written in thread Batman was fictional crime fighting. At the ranch as we had that party show with tv in 2020 The two discoveries marveled my day and enthusiasm. Doing this will keep me going. I only wish for the best for me in this coming year. I was at the station when the phone rang and it was for me. It was Elaine, a counselor calling about my prescription from Dr. Shatterhand. She told me she didn't have it. I told her I remembered giving the prescription to Mrs. Keyes, our house manager. The phone rang again, and again it was for me because I was getting popular around the station.

This time it was Rosemary. She asked the same question, where was my prescription? I told her for sure they had it. I get edgy when it comes to missing medications. I still live with ups and downs. I am not worried about going psychotic on the job or anything, but it becomes obvious, my ups and downs. I take my medications diligently, I hope they find my prescription. I guess my mood swings occur over feeling hypochondriac and allowing myself to miss meds. On the weekend Tony asked me, "What are we going to do?" I knew what he meant. He said, ``What are we going to do with the automobile? I got mad and said, "You mean what am I going to do?" I paid the insurance for the car. For me, the buddy-buddy era is over. Jamal doesn't like to hear arguments or get involved in fights; he just likes to watch television. I can understand. At the onset of these group home experiences and my prior hospital stays, I too would hide myself on television. That was the day though when TV had some decent programming. Not anymore Tony and I feel free to bicker because Tony is semi-tough and bigger than me, but I am a friend to him. We always forgive each other after verbally sparring. The three of us waited around in our room together for the soda and coffee the new guy from the next room over had gone shopping for. My side of the room features an always-made bed, a fish tank with angelfish in it, and a painting of water lilies I did, hung on the wall. I also keep a few books around, some Plaster of Paris sculptures, and a fiber-optic lamp for viewing. Jamal keeps a messy bed with toiletries and a laundry basket scattered around. Tony has a stereo, Rock posters on the wall, and a few Playboy magazines. The three of us are all different. "That guy's taking a long time with that coffee," Jamal said. "What?" Tony asked. Jamal repeated himself, then added, "You'd think he'd be back by now." "Relax you guys, the guy hasn't been gone that long," I said. "You fellows can't agree on whether to have music or sports on TV anyway, so relax" I thought about all the foul language like "Fu k" and "God damn" I heard at the station. I try to keep an open mind, though I can't tolerate it well. A blessed man's language is okay. I talked about foul language and I was warned by one of my residence counselors not to say anything nasty in return. Another reason I want to live in my own place is to avoid so many people crammed together. It is a real dilemma, staying in the group home or moving into my own apartment. It is better to get away from a lot of disillusioned and despondent people. Jamal, Tony, and I are making a great team in these close confines. I have not lived alone before, but I am sure it will work out. But living here at Spring Lake Ranch is becoming almost too comfortable. My meals are prepared for me and my general well-being is kept in line. But I will move on to a single residence occupancy The vacation in March to the family co-op excites me. I'll be totally up for kicking back in those green mountains there.

* * *

It is the Martin Luther King Jr. holiday again. Another MLK Day holiday has arrived, and by Saturday everything was covered in snow. By the end of the weekend, I had accumulated as many chores as there was white stuff on the ground. I was the chef for Sunday. I cooked steak, French fries, and corn. My other chore was washing the kitchen floor all for the others and, since I cooked, I also had to do the dishes. So much for being a real independent. I was the chef and the cleanup. Sunday was also the birthday of one of the residence's women. We all pitched in and got a chocolate cake for her. Other than that, the routine remains the same around here. Jamal watched television most of the day. I went to the shops for coffee and went to the station to feed Casey. Tony slept.

After that, my roommates and I remained quiet, for the most part. "Hi, Jim, I'm going to watch TV," Jamal said. Surprise, surprise, I thought. Like I said, "the routine remains the same." Early in this New Year, circa February 2020 after the MLK holiday, came some new developments. My car insurance check went in the mail. I was accepted to a correspondence school, breaking into Print, acknowledging the acceptance but mailing them a refusal note. I thought I'd do it but did not. I had painted three new paint-by-numbers paintings. I enrolled in a course entitled, "Literary Film," at the local university. Completing this course will finally give me a college degree, a Bachelor of Science. The signs of a new spring were showing, with a few sprouts of daffodils springing up. One of the paintings I had already given to my Dad as a Christmas present, and the other I donated to the Chinese auction at the local Methodist church I belong to. It will probably snow again, but with record temperatures of 68 to 70 degrees, it feels warm and the days are getting longer. It is Groundhog Day and the local ecology center proclaimed that the winter would be longer. They have a real groundhog there. After dinner I drove over to a department store to go shopping with George, again. I asked a clerk where the arts and crafts section was, so I could buy some more paint by numbers kits. I asked some customer service lady about latch hooks. She was a store representative. She mistakenly showed me to the wrong counter. "Oops, right church, wrong pew," she joked. She had that right, I laughed. George and I looked around for different things. At work today, I was elated to hear that the owners were bringing in about a quarter-million dollars a year. Hooray, I chimed to myself, if they bring in that much money, they can certainly pay me a thousand dollars a month. Today was payday and that made me happy. It also happens to be a beautiful Friday, weather-wise. I am making an excited plan to vacation with Eileen. What a real joy this job has been for me, what with all the money I am making. The expense scale is much heavier now because I have to maintain my car, gasoline, and maintenance, etc. And of course, I have to pay the insurance premiums once a year. That covers the bases for me. I still get an allowance and government check once a week, plus another monthly insurance check, and of course the pay I make at work. Some money is better than no money.

* * *

Now it's President's Day weekend. The temperature earlier today was 60 degrees. The temperature went high for the middle of the afternoon. The bright sunshine at its zenith was hitting nothing but blue sky. My small circle of friends includes my one roommate, Jamal Tony, and my girlfriend, Eileen, they are all busy with their usual Saturday routines. I had spent the night before sleeping with the latter. Now Eileen was most likely calling her mother and telling her about our planned trip. That morning I went to my new film class. The film the professor showed us, Smoke Signals and lectured us, which we then were quick to point out the pressure point inside. It burst my bubble, suffice it to say. Then we watched Diva, a French film that had a really good car scene that showed the car going off a bridge into the river. Having a three-day weekend will give me a lot of time to catch up on painting, Plaster of Paris sculpting, writing and reading, and also to do some laundry. Doing so many small projects at once makes me want to reach the top of a mountain. Finally it was time for our holiday, and my girl Eileen's planned vacation weekend. Eileen and I left together on a Friday after work by car. My car. The trip would take about three hours and a half. When we reached White River Junction, we stopped for a break to take a bathroom stop, then got on the road again and drove on to the Valley exit. The ride had breathtaking scenery: big mountains covered with brilliant white snow and winding roads lined by grassy knolls wavering in the brezzes fitted of frozen icicles. We took Route 100 into the actual valley, where we arrived around 11 p.m. First, you go up a hill about a half a mile and then the road slopes down and to the left. The co-op is a flat-roofed multiple dwelling and our family's dwelling sits in the middle. I parked the Elantra under the co-op's overhang. The entrance to the co-op is deeper under the cover of the overhang. We walk through the door into the living room, which has a couch and a small dining table. The tiny kitchen juts off to the side and a stairway leads to a lower level room with bunk beds and a double bed. Even with the upstairs and downstairs combined, the co-op is small. But I like to call it "cozy." I said to Eileen,

"Wait until you see the outside view in daylight." Seeping into her and from the way her eyes took in the place, she seemed to really like it. It was her first visit in spring season, and the second time I had ever brought a girlfriend and only her there. Eileen checked the cupboards. "We'll have to go grocery shopping tomorrow," she said. "Sure we can. Eileen, you can put your bags in the bunk bedroom downstairs," I said. "Remember, the stairs are steep, though, so watch your step, and your head." Eileen hunched over a bit to make it down the stairs with her bags. It was getting late, so we got ready for bed and crawled into the double bed and fell fast asleep. In the morning, I was up at my usual time of 7 a.m. and went upstairs to be alone in the kitchen with the nostalgia I always feel when I first arrive at the co-op. So many memories I have leaning against that kitchen counter. I could hear Eileen still sleeping downstairs. What to do now? I said to myself. I know: Stop playing. Do the chores. Do what you have to do to keep the place clean. It isn't all fun here, you have to sweat a little to have that fun. Perspiration before inspiration. There is the heating to monitor, kitchen chores to do, linen to clean, and, of course, all the vacuuming. I was impressed when Eileen, still bleary-eyed, trudged up the stairs, ready to help out. I was here to enjoy my holiday from the gas station, so I would accept all the help she might offer. I wouldn't pressure her to really do any chores, but I knew she was going to be a great help. Eileen stared out the window of the living room upstairs "What a marvelous view," she said, opening her eyes wide and stretching out with a yawn. "You are looking at Sugarbush mountain," I said. "Gorgeous," Eileen said. "Eileen, you'll help me keep the place clean while we're here, right?" I inquired of her. "I will help you out to make sure you will have Helen's approval. Fair enough?" "More than fair enough," I said. My sister Gloria lives over the mountain we were both nested on. She owns a coffee shop in the Valley. Her husband, Derek, is a damn good plumber and has a virtual plumbing monopoly in the Valley. He is Austrian, and he and my sister have two grown children, a boy and a girl. I decided that Ellen and I should pay them a visit, since we were just on the other side of the mountain. We stopped in at the coffee shop, a Green Mountain Coffee Roasters franchise, to see her. "Hi Gloria," I said. "Good to see you, Jamie," Gloria replied. "Who's this lovely lady?" "That's Eileen," I said. As my sister and I chatted with each other up, suddenly Eileen wanted to go grocery shopping. I didn't want to go—I mean, shopping can be had anywhere, the valley excitement and dusting of snow mountains can't. I just wanted to buzz around the Valley, try to catch Derek driving around, visit other co-op families, or people I knew in the Valley, like our neighbor Paul. I didn't know if Paul was at the co-op, he might have arrived the other night and already left in the morning but I wasn't sure. After seeing my sister, we drove back to the co-op to do chores so we could go out and have some fun in nature. I couldn't get serious about doing any of these chores, and the truth was, this time out, I was able to. I hoped that Eileen would serve as my co-pilot in the cleaning takeoff so we could fly into the skies of our vacation. "What do you want to do??" I asked Eileen. "I don't know," she answered. "Let me do some cleaning while you think about it." Great! My one taught Prayer answered. It was up to me to figure out the fun, and her to take care of the minor stuff, including the necessary major cleaning. It was a glorious, warm Saturday, so I suggested we go down to the local swimming hole. We dropped what we were doing and drove straight to the river. Eileen wouldn't swim, the water would be too rapid anyway, and I didn't either because it was still only March, or I was sure the water would be cold as an icebox. I pointed out a rock outcropping about thirty feet high. "Eileen, see those rocks?" "Yes, sir, I do," she said. "That's where we use to jump off into the water," I said. Eileen said nothing, just stared into space. "You wouldn't get me to jump off those rocks if you paid me a million bucks, I'd be too afraid," Eileen confided. We got back in the car and drove back. When we got back to the co-op, Eileen said, "Jamie, let's finally do some shopping." "Okay, let's go!" I said, and spun the car back around. Somehow in that small decision, I felt that Eileen was a bit distancing. At the local general store, we got plenty of food—cut meats, eggs, bread, milk, etc., for the weekend. When we got back, Eileen wanted to start cooking, but I suggested we go for a hike instead, to build up our appetites. "Not a long hike," she warned. "No, just up the road a little bit, to build up our appetites," I said. We dropped what we were doing, organizing our food on the counter and gathering the necessary utensils, and headed back outside into the tamed wilderness. Hiking in the crisp fresh green mountain air was refreshing. There was a lot of open space on the hike but it wasn't like our community residence where we were just nested in the woods, here, we were the woods. After the hike, I left Eileen back at the coop coffee shop again. Took the car to my sister. I asked Gloria,

"How are the ski conditions at Mad River Glen?" "Don't know, Jamie, haven't been there at all this winter," she said. "I have been too busy with the shop here." "I gotta get up there," I said. "I want to take Eileen there, show her the mountain." I circled back to the co-op to pick up Eileen, and then realized what a mistake it was to have left her alone at the co-op. The bad event: She had taken a fall down those steep basement stairs and had slightly hurt herself. "You okay?" I asked. "Just a bump on the hip. I'll be fine," she said. Afterward, Eileen and I jumped back in the car and drove up to Mad River's base box and watched all the skiers zigzagging down on their ski runs. I hadn't skied at Mad River for ten years, at least since I was a young man in my early twenties. When I was a twenty-something kid, skiing the "waterfall cutoff," the last trail to the base box was always a huge social event. I had lots of friends then and we all had lots of fun going up on the mountain, on skis or on foot. I was sure that for Eileen, the area was just another ski mountain. To me, it was that special place I came of age, part of the adolescence I overly loved and made myself a very good freestyler. Mad River also symbolized something else because the family co-op is where I had my secondstring (childhood), Then which my head became like the top of a turntable record machine and spun me out of control. But those earliest skiing jaunts and the college stress the disastrous events after my mom passed and I was in a financial and emotional dilemma., are in the past. Eileen and I made dinner that Saturday night and sat before the fire we made in the fireplace. With my arm around her, I pondered whether to take Eileen out into the Valley bar scene, but thought better of it. I love her enough—there, I said it—to just sit and be alone with her without any distractions. We woke up Sunday morning to a day gone cloudy and cold, with about a foot of snow blanketing the ground and weighing down the boughs of all the trees. We went to Catholic Mass at Our Lady of the Snows Church. I think Eileen really enjoyed it, judging by her frequent smiles. After church, we sat around in the living room and got comfortable. For Eileen and for me it was the perfect retreat and just reward for a lot of hard, personal work, sitting there like two old people just spending the day together sitting and staring at the vast and wooded mountain landscape. Then reality struck. It seemed a world away, but the CR home was actually quite close, just over a series of mountain humps whose winding roads only created the illusion of distance. When midafternoon came around, I confessed, really, to Eileen that we'd have to leave soon. All we had to do now was clean up, and Eileen was the real big help she had promised to be, taking the lead so I wouldn't have to. I guess she understood how hard I worked at the station (and at life?). Our family's co-op since it was constructed in 1963 has been in the same condition and still bears the marks of it. Someone who rented there before had wall art on one of the living room walls of a cartoon of two skiers at the top of the lift eager to ski down with the caption (in a bubble): "Go home and face your responsibilities." And we did just that. A saying from the New Yorker magazine.

Minus Ten Degrees
of Uncertainty

In our room, Jamal, Tony, and I are preparing to sleep. "Tony always has that radio on," I discreetly told Jamal. "I'll take care of it," Jamal said and turned to Tony. "Tony, you have to turn off that radio, cuz Jim and I can't sleep. Be a good man." "All right, I'll put the headphones on," Tony said to Jamal. Jamaal had been discharged from the psychiatric ward recently, and I had come home earlier that day to find him smiling in front of the television. He gleefully kept at Tony, "And the dentist called three times for you about your appointment. Don't you want to get your teeth taken care of?" "I have to get some root canals done," Tony replied. "That's what, what I'm talking about," Jamal said couldn't blame Tony for not seeing his dentist—my own (Jamie) dentist had long since given up calling me. Luckily, Billy at the station referred me to a better dentist who happened to accept Medicaid. The next day, Tony asked, "What should we do now?" He never stops hinting about using my automobile. "Tony, how many times do I have to tell you, it's my car, I bought it, I use it when I want and with who I want," I said. I went back to staring at the television.

Reading always lulls me to sleep, as does the bubbling of the aquarium and/ or a dishwasher, Jamal is still busy putting his clothes away, stuffing socks and underwear loosely in his dresser until he is tired enough to try to sleep. I have always been organized and simple about how I keep my belongings, but as for me, it's usually not easy to fall asleep. Sometimes at the Ranch I really have to dissociate my mind because it races. I've got my forward thinking going, so nothing is going to stop me or get in my way. I'm determined to get out, independent and on my own 'dime'. My past taught me to get out before a fall (in the case of waterfalls), so I am doing my best to focus my behavior toward moving out of this government assisted house. The next day, I wake up already scheming about how I'm going to find better employment than the station can offer. Later, I gave Tony and his girl forty-two dollars for a ticket to a concert at the Hartford civic center. They saw Billy Joel in concert. "You get paid today?" Tony asked, just before he left the room. I assumed he wanted to borrow money from me, so I pretended not to hear him. "I am starting a job with a sheltered workshop," Jamal chimed "My counselor at the day treatment center suggested it." "That's good Jamal," I said. While watching television, Jamie speaks up, "I don't expect much out of life! I've tried to become rich and independent but I've been diseased in the mind!" "At least you have a life, Jim!" Jamal said. "Really," Jim answered. My inner thoughts warn me I'll be single all my life. After that Tony flew downstairs, I assumed, straight to the fridge. Tony walked back up the stairs and into the room with a cup in his hand. We hear Elaine's shout, "Tony, did you take a cup up there?" "What if I did?"

Tony said. "Bring it down," Elaine demanded. "It's empty, and besides, it's mine!" Tony retorts. Earlier I had lunch at Domino's Pizza, then settled on my bed in front of the television, the fish aquarium, and the fiber-optics lamp. I watched the BBC News Hour. After the show ended, I jumped in my car and traveled over to Eileen's to spend Saturday night. She had prepared supper and by the time I arrived, she had already filled her dining table with steak, potatoes, and green beans. "Jamie I'm so proud of you for working so hard to move forward," she said over bites of steak. "You've really got it all together now." I laughed between my own bites of steak. "I'm happy to hear you feel that way," I couldn't help but say. What I really love about Eileen is her open, sweet, and kind heart. I left Eileen's for Spring Lake Ranch with a magnificent last-ditch cheer of a sunset at my back. I still had to take out the garbage, take my medications, and do my laundry. As I stepped in the door, Jamal grabbed me. "Eileen just called you." "When did she call?" I asked. "I was just at her place." "Like I said, before you got home," Jamal said. Eileen was obviously looking for me, but for some strange reason she didn't call me on my cell, she called me on the common area payphone. I was ready and going to return her call. Now it's Saturday and the weather is absolutely beautiful, and I had a lot to accomplish. The only problem, one I didn't concern myself too much over, was that I didn't tell my father about my whereabouts. I started out the day at school. I got my first two assigned papers back, both critiques of that French film, Diva. I did fine on the exams. After school, I checked on the station dog, fed him, and filled up the car's gas tank. Then I drove to west Springfield to get a haircut. A quick drive back to the YMCA saw me swimming once again in its indoor pool. I did a quarter-mile, got dressed and drove back to the public library near the high school. There I made a copy of my photograph that landed me a prize way back when I lived in Greenwich. I also checked out a book, "Harry and Tonto Fistfight in Heaven." Once I finally settled back at the Ranch, Jamal informed me that Helen had called me. After everything I had accomplished that day, the senior generation of my family expected that after school I'd help them in their garden, so where the heck was I? I explained what I had been doing all day and promised I'd come to help out the next weekend. Fine by them. I already do plenty of chores at the Ranch. Everyone here is required to do a single, individual job each day. It's toward our "betterment." We chop wood to build up our physical strength and supply heat for winter. We also clean the bathroom loos and sinks and do the dishes. I do a lot of solo work for myself, as well. I clean my aquarium, the water tank outdoors with a garden hose, then the bathtub itself, which is always dirty and filled with everyone's hair. I keep my side of the room very organized, with the bed made, and every stitch of clothing in its proper place. In fact, last Saturday night, no one needed to tell me to mop the kitchen floor, I just did it. I need and want to have a good job: I not only do the chores I'm asked to do, but I also go the extra mile. What cost me money and why I haven't saved more are my running all those errands and friend loans, which equates to losing out. I should keep to the chores because they are generally free and I actually enjoy them. I'd like to drop forty pounds. Once upon a time, I was in good shape, but these days it's not easy for me.

I've been snacking too much lately. I like drinking beer, and that tobacco snuff habit still snatches me too often. I know alcohol and meds don't mix. Jim has to be as diligent on this danger as that of any illicit drug or drug of "The Man." One job that Jim (after a name change from Jamie) ought to get paid for, so all residents say and agree, is just all the chores I do. I am the type of person most get along with, so people say: "not so much "Jim says humbly. Come Monday, rain fell in the morning and the sun snuck out from behind a cloud, but then it was hidden to leave the day overcast. I did my job as a responsible resident and went back to my corner by the windows and did some writing. "Jim, aren't you taking a big risk by working at your paying job," Tony said. "What work are you talking about Tony?" I hammered back. "They could kick you out of the program!" Tony said. It's true there are income limits when a person collects Social Security disability, but I like to work as much as I can. Come Wednesday after dinner, Jamal had finished his turn at washing clothes, and was stuffing—literally—his dried clothes away when I walked into the room. "I heard something," Jamal said to me. "What'd you hear?" I said. "That you have an athlete's foot," he said. "Yes, that must be it," I answered. I thought, it's more like an Achilles heel named Orion, and I laughed under my breath.

What, besides a humorous tone, It always caused Jamal such anguish and boredom when he changed his linen, Why I will never know. "I am going to put Batman on again later," Tony said from bed. He even started to sing the Batman theme! Jamal shoves his dresser doors in. "Finally got my clothes done," he said. We discussed some early schooling books like

Jonathan Livingston Seagull and Jamal suggests what we ought to do for the next Halloween. "I don't want to be the Devil again, because that's what our counselor Rose is going to be," Jamal jokes. Mrs. Rose Keyes is our lead counselor, and she already resembles the Devi he joked again. By Halloween, we all know Thanksgiving and Christmas will come next. Isn't all of this life worthy of holidays? I thought. We spent most of the rest of the night talking about baseball. The three of us became ambivalent about whether we should watch Batman again—or The World According to Jim, or The Jamie Foxx Show, for that matter. I'd prefer to watch baseball, at least tonight, even though Jim really had little interest in watching TV at all. Meeting adjourned. "We have to forfeit some things in life." Jamie suddenly chimed. "Why do you say that?" Jamal asked. "Jamie will give up the radio and the boom box to read and write on paper," I said. Tony decided to leave the room altogether to go outside and smoke a cigarette. I went to the counselors' office to get my mail, where I received another letter from Helen:

> I hope you are enjoying your Saturday morning film/ literature course. Do not just pick book titles that you have already read. After all, college is supposed to expand your knowledge. So do not take the easy way through. We thought that you might have called in at least once this spring, so we missed you. Enclosed are a couple of pay-in slips. Keep them in a safe place.

Well, my dear, take care of yourself and we will speak to, or better, see you soon.

Love,
Helen

This was the empathetic letter I received after having missed the weekend at Sunset Bluff. Spring Lake Ranch houses mostly psychiatrically challenged people, but there are healthy people here too, as well as some disabled. Spring Lake Ranch will be discharging me soon because I seem to have become not only calmer, but my calamity is gone. Lately, I am in love with my own good mood as much as I am with Eileen. A good mood is a much healthier mood to have. I take an empowerment self-test every day so I can continue better behavior than I exhibited in prior years. I am still not very good at social grace, that "stick with it," ethic and my personal metabolism, but I'm getting better. My job pumping gas, putting my education first, and sticking with psychological therapy—it all helps. Moving to my own apartment would be the best phase I could enter now. In my mind Lately I've found a midpoint. I feel I'll be okay. My last chores of the night were to dust the woodwork and wash the telephone mouthpiece, and yes, washing the telephone mouthpiece is a real job around the Ranch. Doing my chores, just like I do with my favorite TV show, completely shelves me for the day. This daily test of theatrics is not enough anymore. Everyone has to remain "cool" enough for their daily tests. I am soon to be a degree holder, and my mind tends to center around many courses (careers). If I don't become really successful in occupation or just living in mankind. I am still fighting to try it. If at first I didn't succeed I will try, try again.

* * *

It was another Saturday, in May, with a blue sky and sunny morning sunny weather. Shining in my classes in the library I drove to class in my Hyundai, then I drove from the Ranch to the station to feed Casey and fill up the tank again. I then drove to Greenwich to help out my family at Sunset Bluff. That's lots of driving. They, Helen and Dad were already cutting the grass, and I jumped right into the garden weeding. We took a break to eat lunch and I prepared to go over with Helen to the old digs here, the house that I used to stay and board at before the Ranch, to coiffed the garden and smarten up the lawn. I swept the sidewalk then Dad and I threw fertilizer around, then I edged the garden and cut some brown branches off the evergreen. I look, Dad had a big black eye that I woke up from my work and saw! "What happened to your eye, Dad?" I asked. "Ah, it's nothing, I just fell into an unmarked man-hole at a construction area and hit my face." My old man said it asks if such things happened to him every day. I was awfully worried about my father's age and physical condition. At least if God takes him away, say, sucks him into a deeper manhole, he'll be forever at peace. And no longer have to worry about me. I was a pain-in-the-ass to my old man in life. I began out as a good kid but they tell me I had mumps-meningitis at two years old and had to be put in a bucket of ice water. The consequences of that I couldn't see growing up. It is a neurological disease of temporary measures. If I'd stuck to methodology in all facets of doing things in life I might have avoided the social/psychological path. There is a method to doing all things in life, the right way.

* * *

After helping out at Sunset, I drove back to the Ranch and made a steak and soup dinner. Then I cleaned my little corner of the room and took my laundry to the basement wash. I took off the dirty black trousers I'd been wearing all day, put them in with a wad of other colored clothes, and snuck back to my room in my skivvies. A lady who lives in the house saw the tail end of me, but she didn't even flinch. She grunted. In this beautiful two-story house, I've lived in for seven years now, none of us have enough eyes to witness every activity that goes on downstairs, but someone always lets us know if we're required to do anything Otherwise, we are free to do our own thing. I was on my back on my bed still in my skivvies when I said to Tony, "Tony, you don't seem happy?" "What do you mean?" he asked. The phone downstairs had been ringing for about five minutes. "The telephone. You don't answer it?" Before he could answer, I thought, all of us have cell phones now, so why is there still a public payphone in the residence foyer? "Yo," Tony finally replied and began to move his things around here and there and shut off his radio, doing his best to deny the ringing of the phone. Yo, is an urban statement or a response that really expresses no opinion and is just another redundant way to address somebody about something. "And then there's the dishes," I said. "Yo," Tony said. "The dishes just sit there, getting dirtier and dirtier to jab". It's not my chore," I got to call Eileen. The sink," I continued Now I'm at the Spring Lake Ranch kitchen waiting for Jamal to come back. When he does, I'm planning to say, "Did you visit your psychiatrist yet?" I know he did, but I just want to rub it in. I feel like some evil jockey for mocking him, but I don't really understand why he is in such a revolving door with the hospitals. Another housing would be a really sweet arrangement if I could live by myself in a peaceful room with no blaring radio or television. I'm dreaming, because I'm still stuck on my Ranch bed in my shared room, with nothing to do at present but focus on the swoosh of Tony's Nike cap. At the end of every work day, and always on my bed in the corner, I consider how the day went, reminding myself over and over how laid back I really am and easy to make friends with. In any schooling I've had, so far I've never cheated, which also makes me basically honest. It enters my mood how to best let go of my past and change my worst habits: the gambling and bars and lazy ethic. I have to keep my short-term memory sharp and put the past out of my head, I think to myself, though I'm sure most adults think this, too. The last book I read, Sherman Alexie's The Lone Ranger and Tonto Fistfight in Heaven, is the last story I have to read in my college lit class. Other books we have read are, To Kill a Mockingbird, and Iron and Silk. My class also watched the corresponding movie to Alexie's book, "Smoke Signals." When the next Wednesday rolled around, Jamal asked me, "Jim, would you like to go see a movie at my mother's country club?" "When, Jamal?" I asked. "Thursday night," he replied. "Want to go?" "Let me see how I feel after pumping gas all day tomorrow," I said. We never went to the movies. "Jim," Tony said. "I have to go get more cigarettes." "Oh really? I suppose you expect me to drive you to the store to get some." "Yeah," he replied. "Alright, Tony, guess what? Next Saturday, I'll drive you to the Indian reservation to get some when I get a chance. Later that day, Tony and I walked to the local 7--11 and he talked about his wish to have a car of his own and about his ideas on loving women. "I'd like to get a car someday, too," he said. "What kind?" I asked. "The car in Dukes of Hazzard: The General Lee" "Good choice," I said. "Jim?" "Yup?" "I hope you don't get annoyed by driving me to get smokes," Tony said. "Once in a while is fine," I replied. "I'd get a wife in a heartbeat if I was the one driving," Tony said. I didn't say much. Later that day at counseling, Elaine asked me during my therapy session, "Tell me your feelings." I did not smirk and told her I was feeling a good, and a humorous mood coming on. I was really quite pleased with my progress and my work and schooling. "I have to get an easier but better paying job soon," I said. "Pumping gas gives me a lot of experience with people, but I stand around, and then move, then stand around, etc. No problem I will walk into selling Insurance policies!" The biggest excitement to be had there is handling the money." Elaine widened her eyes. "The obvious problem is I have to give it to the owner," I confessed. "Very interesting," she said, grinning and making a note. What I didn't mention to her—was that all that oil changing, flat fixing, and engine starting I do was really the best part of work because it allowed me to work with the same routine, so I can eventually "stick with" and gain skills with whatever I attempt in the future. Another reality about pumping gas and doing productive work with your hands is that it can tire you out, and getting tired can also be a stabilizer. The truth is, at this point, now that I'm getting closer to being released, the questions the social counselors asked questions are becoming a bit redundant: Are you a harm to yourself? Are you a harm to others? Do you feel symptoms or hear voices? "No, no, undoing but spending another day watching television! 77 I like these guys, my roommates Tony and Jamal, mind you, we can all trust one another. I can leave money out in the open with no worry about it going missing, though what money I've made I've mostly spent and not put away in the bank. But I wised up and I have a safe that I put all my valuables in when I enter my room and I put a padlock on my door because people can and have done pick the lock. No more smelling of gas and oil. I'd feel anything...but with Eileen there was talk. Eileen and Jamie were planning to take a kind of elope and to the co-op with all our stuff and get away from the Spring lake ranch. and her housing. This would be was a rash move and I never even followed through with transferring the government assisted rental money to help us out and get going. If at the co-op, I'd start to research class c mechanic work. In the middle of summer most garages were full with employees. For months I keep looking and probably I would trout fish a lot. For Eileen, I think she'd appreciate bunking together, she'd be glad to also be away from her residents, but in conclusion all I say is it was talk. My brother, and my father and I tended to have really far-fetched ideas at times. This was a perfect example.

Great Scott!
What Happened?

I'll most likely be paying rent all my entire life. I am destined for Southold, in Long Island, New York. It promises to be a better place, and the second level of housing. I am now in a better economic/ status. At the meeting of Dawn, and the one other female friend of Tony. There have been erotic and sometimes heated up feelings between us. Jim's focus is out of vices, a minimum of alcohol and in like putting time on work and keeping it which has been fun and satisfactory in many ways. And Jim's holding down a job as a driver for now. I began dating Dawn. I don't believe that Tony knew but he might be aware. I was paying bills even through tough ways with Dawn and gambling /bars, etc. now out. Dawn came on to me in the midst of all social gatherings at Spring lake ranch. In the shuffle of moving from the Spring Lake Ranch to across the state. I had a lot of things to do and I'd rented a U-Haul and left my car at the garage. As I packed and prepared, on a weekend overnight the Hyundai Elantra was stolen! It so happened that while I was asleep, someone had taken the keys to my personal car and went for a joy ride. I was in such shock that night, I looked out my door into the driveway and yelled where is the car? Jim sat stumped in his sitting room, completely baffled but never relinquished hope. I ran out in the night from the residence in the dodge dart and raced down the road. I took many roads, hopefully looking to see and catch my Hyundai. I kept driving until I saw the new dawn and a new day. I thought, what if the car is totaled? Before the night trip finished, about 7 am the police came to my door and said they had found the car. "Is it totaled": I asked. "No" You can pick it up, it is drivable and parked in a police impound near back bay station in Boston. Well that mishap occurred between just about the time I would be moving out and into independent housing from 24/7 to Southold. I didn't need this. Where and who got access to my keys? By then they (the police) were neither figuring Eileen nor I. It was a real hassle for six weeks. I had to ride my bicycle to work 10 miles every day, the car was repaired to class A1 condition, the culprit will be caught. If so he/she will be found guilty of grand larceny and justice will prevail. I received a letter from the District Attorney. The letter claimed they were investigating the man/woman who was involved, there was no suspicious incident "I" was involved in, but the letter concerned me.

To the person of question:

To date we have been unsuccessful in our attempts to contact you regarding your stolen vehicle. We ask that you contact this office upon receipt of this letter. If we do not hear from you within fifteen days of this letter we will assume you are not presenting a claim and we will close our file. It is incumbent upon you to use this opportunity to clear up this matter.

D.A.

A few days later they called. I never had to file a theft report. The state took care of it. In my new resident home so far I have been fine with my moving on. I have moved on to the south across the border into another state. The new resident house in Southold is a big one with a large backyard and plenty of space. I always kept my space clean back at Spring Lake Ranch, and now that I'm at this new space, I still keep my room clean, fresh smelling and picked up and have gotten used to also cleaning the bathroom and the kitchen, and vacuuming the rug often. and have a small garden plot.

One evening out in the surrounding neighborhood, I met this woman, Cassandra. "Think about what you can do with what you already hold," she said during our conversation. Oddly, as odd as my whole social helping workers experiences, I had already dreamt these sage words the previous night. Cassandra was going off to an interview that day, and I hung around long enough to speak about random things with her before she left. "Just be yourself in the interview. Tell your potential employer that you just have to pay your mortgage." My words were no match for believability. Just be honest with your interviewer." A few days passed and I meet Cassandra again. The first words out of her mouth were, "I got hired! The advice that you gave me before I left for the interview was just right. They created a positive aura for me!" "What kind of job did you get hired for?" I asked. "You must be thrilled!" "I am now a counselor at a group rehabilitation home," she said. My jaw almost fell to my feet. It just felt good to speak up about something for somebody and it had been so easy. I didn't have to get cocky, I was just proud to offer this little advice about honesty, putting my inborn common sense to good use. I was truly glad for Cassandra. Kicking back in my new living room I felt a little less narcissistic but prouder. I look out the window, eating bites of a pie I had made, and decide to call about my time at the CR in Spring Lake Ranch and maybe reach Tony. Lo and behold, of course Tony did answer the phone this time. "Hi, Tony, how are you? I guess you're in a better mood," I said. "Why do you say that? Jim! What are you doing, man?" Tony asked. "I am eating a piece of strawberry-rhubarb pie that I made." Then Tony said, "Oh yeah? Becoming a pie master now? I've been going to work three days a week." "Unbelievable. Good for you," I said. "How's Jamal?" "Jamal ain't all right, he's been transferred to an adult home over in St Albans.," Tony said. We chatted a bit more and then with bitter screaming and cursing we had our finally. It was he who had stolen the car. Everything was coming out in the laundry wash. Next I tried to get a hold of Jamal, but he couldn't be reached at his new place. In theory, climbing up that first set of steps out of a group home life took me to the second floor, but I still knew I'd be climbing more sets of steps in the future. To what floor in life would such steps lead, I didn't know precisely but leaning to independence. Reminiscing, there was one Sunday that summer on this second floor in the ranch, when I devoted an entire day toward sharpening my painting skills. During a break, three other residents George, Glen, and I took a walk to the grocery store in the shopping center of downtown Springfield. When we arrived, we saw police cars overtaking the parking lot. I looked ahead from our approaching stroll and saw a liquor store with a smashed-out glass door. Word around the vicinity was that someone had stolen the store's supply of lottery tickets. I guess the culprit wanted to make himself one lucky chap. Since we were approaching a liquor store, I begged Tony—I don't believe in his habit, but I am sure he could use some cigarettes, and they usually sell one vice alongside other vices. When I saw the price it was outrageous. My common sense came in handy in this situation, and, as far as my own non-smoking is concerned, has always come in handy. Nearing home again with the things we purchased, the sun is shining brightly over the open landscape enclosing my ex-residence home with tree-filled woods. Monday came up very suddenly. I looked up at my temperature gauge, a new thermostat, and it was already 86 degrees by eleven o'clock in the morning. There was no longer a need to go to the station on weekends to take care of Casey, because he's dead. He was really just the bosses' filling station watchdog, but I liked seeing him every day and I miss him. Outside my new window tower are huge oak and maple trees. Just looking up at them waggles in a breeze. It's a Tuesday evening and the leaves are falling around from the changing season. Rabbits and squirrels race around the landscape, anticipating sunset. Easy chairs line the verandah and invite the residents to sit and chat, which they do. When the evening approaches, the glow of lightning bugs flying around the woods mirrors the glow of residents lighting up their cigarettes on the veranda. The sun casts its long beams down on our residence and sinks into the western sky over the horizon. "Clean up for fifteen minutes each day" was our motto. "The best time to clean up is in the morning." Here in the anew my motto is my scripture, if I don't attend dinner, I eat fast food. Chores like doing the laundry or the dishes are small problems. Scrubbing the interior dirt and cleaning the house gutters of leaves and grass can be a major job, however. Keep up the positive mood, Jim, even though mechanics won't be your future vocation. Yes I will, I'll keep working at some work.

* * *

When I settle and work landscaping and driving in Southold, I'll return to using computers, and I even picked up the new hobby of studying "Soh-cah-toa," a new spin on mathematics. It is a kind of computer game that challenges your math aptitudes. I also like crossword puzzles and scrabble are fun for me. I am also relearning the college calculus that I now seem to be mastering (always got A's in math at school). And also, skimming with vectors which is application of math and physics. On Wednesday, it was sunny and I got another buzz haircut, and it was, again, great for me. The wonders a new haircut can do, especially when the hot and humid summer hits. Not coincidentally the maintenance-free buzz haircut means little need for much, if any, shampoo as I can shave and shower with regular soap to save myself some cash. Most folks around here are not so keenly aware that we are really, despite the surroundings, living like paupers. I am quite looking forward to finding new work, and along with it feeling humbly fit and maybe some new friends. We are poor albeit fit in the sense that we just rent and pay bills with a little left aside. As I lie on my new bed, thinking about the day's events and the past several years in general, I feel humbly fit. I look up at my photograph on my windowsill, a happy picture of a man working at pumping gas that appeared in the county art display. I am trying to pinpoint who's in the picture with me and my car when I recalled the photograph of the Greenwich prize. Only a handful of my own friends knew about this work I did and where I got my first car. The day the picture was taken, I remember well. I had spent the whole damn day in 99-degree heat pumping gas ten years ago, and let me tell you, it wasn't at all pleasant seemingly until I had four days off and Eileen and I spent the time at the co-op. Eileen telephoned just shortly to say she was feeling much better. She was recently in a psych ward. I would have visited her, but I refused at the time. She was staying in Hartford State Hospital, but only for a short time. I love her, but Eileen had no good avenues to drive in her life. She was struck down by depression, and I thought she would be well in the Clubhouse, but afterward, she swore to never go there again, so I don't know at all. Stay all along the watchtower! Clean occasionally? When she's in that big house in Springfield, all she does is trudge around and mope and that brings me down. I can no longer rely on her for encouragement. Nowadays, only Dad and Helen encourage me. With them, I have true mentors. When Eileen last telephoned, she sounded a little better, which made me glad. The fact that I have been driving has made a huge difference in our relationship. I'm sure Eileen would love me to take her to one of the beaches, like a Long Island Beach. I'm not sure, I know because she'd already asked me. I would like to plan a long car trip, a "road trip," also. Like the co-op trip again.

I might be working at the local Carnival this Fourth of July, and the country fair is only a short ride from Southold, so it could be a lot of fun to work there as well., I need time work as much as the next guy. Back in Springfield as one final memory, we residents seemed to be getting to know each other so well that we are able to pick up most of the slack in our conversations. One night at the residence meeting, we all had each other laughing and joking over what to have for gaming as we were to have fowl for dinner. Duck, duck, or goose! I pretended to run and hide my head like a goose, only allowing myself to take a "gander" at the room. I came back to my room to turn on the radio just before I walked into our little hamper room to organize my clothes. "That's totally ridiculous. You are not to listen to my radio," Tony said "You know you are gonna get it," I said, after a pause. "Oh yeah? I don't want anything to do with it." Everybody loves that radio as much as I do. "What's wrong with what I did, Jim?" I questioned out loud. "Well, you just look like you were asking to get into trouble by picking up that damn stereo." I answered myself. "No, I am doing fine." The fact is, Rock and roll is dead and is a catalyst to my demise. I believe in emulating TV actors. Racing engines are what feelings sound like. Car drivers are loud so others, and pedestrians can hear them coming (for safety) in a conglomerate area. For our cities, this protagonist said "wow", a change in growth from small town escapes to city's living, is almost a culture shock to an indigenous / ordinary man.

Prisoner of Love

There are no friends from my past that we still talk or socialize with, yet apartment living and Social Security benefits accountability completely cut (and a wait until I am 70) I am leaving Eileen and that's made me down in the dumps, but I am still keeping my chin up. On this four-day weekend, I went to a pig roast in the upstate mountains near the town of Springfield and saw my now ex-woman Eileen at the house she's been staying in. She kept approaching me, repeating, "You look good. You look good." We sat around and I took in the state of the house: definitely in need of painting and touch-ups, a bunch of light bulbs inside needed to be replaced but the "garden and yard" is where the real problems appeared. It had long uncut grass, weeds overgrown and limbs scattered all over the yard from the last major storm. I am better off but unlovely since Eileen would not let me move somewhere closer to her. But all she could muster was a day rehabilitation center. She and I discussed things with Eileen and Jim "We just haven't been ourselves," Jim told Eileen. "And I heard about your telephone conversation with Helen." The two women had been at a vineyard in Greenwich with a dress – and-ladies kind of show or affair. Apparently, there had been no talk about her and I visiting any beaches. After the drive-up Interstate 91 to where I had first visited Eileen and we had spent that weekend in the mountains, I had started feeling enumerated (like giving) financially again. I veered the conversation toward the scenario of our love. "I have taken you to concerts, as well as to the store many times. I have taken you on vacation and to the ball games. Eileen, what have you done for me?" I said. "Think about it." "The All-Star Game is on tonight!" was her only reply. "I love baseball." "Oh yeah, what time?" I asked. "Eight o'clock," she said. "I'll put the game on now!" she said, and got up to run in the house. "Eileen, we were talking about our situation. To hell with baseball!" I said and got up to leave. There is a new treatment on the market and it is called Neurostar. The simple Painless procedure has very effective and positive results for treating major depression in Adults. We never discussed using Neurostar for either Eileen or I. In these days treatment Centers, it is not used, not even displayed nor discussed by these mental health professionals. Well, Eileen may be a good candidate, but we were finished. I just wish the best for her only. And I am certainly not going for Neurostar treatment. One thing that is different on Smith road is that the population living in Southold here (in per square mile) is denser than Springfield's, where sometimes you wouldn't see people around for miles.

People will always be difficult in your face, and if I could place myself in their shoes or maybe think empathetically, I have to empower and work on my own self-respect self, Well, one aspect about my behavior other people would probably mention about me if asked would be, "Jim only cares about how good a room is picked up, how clean and smooth-running a car is, that his clothes are washed and that one's body I kept clean." There's food, too, of course, "And that he doesn't know how to cook very well." What's for dinner? I questioned myself. I think I'll make fish filets and fries after eating dinner and watching television all night, Jim finally fell asleep. The diggs I rent here at Southold holds a beauty, yet it's in better condition than any other of my previous living arrangements. These days, what I care about most: making sure the rent gets paid every month, With a heart of glass it is now full with water for Jim's heart. Provincially, upstanding against many diverse ethnicities puts me in an omnipotent mood initially but it wears down, But thinking out of the box…Others probably see me as "asserting myself, what doesn't kill me will only make me stronger, and don't mistake my kindness for weakness." so ridding myself of that "nice guys always finish last" mind-set,. Some of the past problems were that he's too trusting and he used to take a bath financially. Jim is seemingly coming into a new way. It was a harrowing night ride in the 14 Honda with Dawn in the car. We were going to have dinner. During the ride she began popping Many clozapine and I tried to stop her. She also opened the passenger car door while we were doing 60 mph. "What the f--K are you doing?" I yelled "Close that!" When we arrived she bex\came very quiet so much so that it was a worry. She had begun to OD, I called 911 and the ambulance and she was rushed to the hospital. The next day she was released and was okay And I was finished with that relationship/. To the point where now I care for her. The side romance with Dawn, and only affair turned out to be a really bad love, and consequently continued getting even worse. It can be a quick and hasty end. I just didn't believe in her enough. She was facing so many days, even months of recovery, which frustrated James enough to break it off. End it immediately for God's sake and her illicit gatherings could have winded me up in jail. Jim was still exercising his own diligence bringing equilibrium to his own mind about work and he didn't have enough stamina (confidence lapses) such as pushing the trouble out of the way. Without her will make for a real exciting future. Yo with the little psychological attributes Jim developed, a coping mechanism could just about prove as good a head on the shoulders as that of all, or many peers in our psycho-sociological sphere of acquaintances. Dawn used me with her manipulating and Tony would not even care or probably didn't know of our love affair.

* * *

Since the State job offers me NYSHIP health insurance with free vision and dental benefits, I am making good use of those, I am a union member as well. Those benefits will be in my possession for a long time to come. I spent a long time under the shadow of my father's super successful career. I had plotted a niche in me that one day I'll be a happy homeowner and not government– dependent. and it sticks with me: how long a personal issue can hang around Yet, although the opportunity is there, I see the world is changing around all of us. The new changes are reflecting in me, maybe I had all I needed right there in the agency and living on social security. Lately the many people state and have told me, you are doing well and you look happier. If I want to stop the psych meds I see nothing wrong with that. I did condone with my regular psychiatrist that albeit I need the meds, my fate and destiny tells me. Yet I want more out of life, period. Spring arrived late and the last weeks of March suffered many snowstorms. The way we were taught: there'd been an agricultural revolution, then an industrial development to finally come to a time revolution. What we got though was an information technology blast. Where does that lead to? The world in which I was reared in was a different time, an old era. Accomplishing this new residence makes me damn proud. I gave up any lingering dream I had of trying my hand at computer programming because computer specialist jobs are just too intricate and tricky on a personal computer regarding the expenses they accrue. Besides that, the many times I applied for computer work, I never even got a response letter! They just didn't reply! I also gave up the election board work I worked at for a few times per year. I gave up on insurance. I have the privilege of two licenses: one: a life insurance broker and two: an accident and health broker. I am content to be a housekeeper here at a job and then at my house. With retirement coming in less than a year I have very few worries about meeting goals /expenses. I choose to live alone.

My Way Is to Trust and Obey

The forsythia are starting to bloom, and some daffodils are springing up. Inside the apartment, my new pet cat, Boo boo, is lazily resting, a daily occurrence now. I guess Boo boo is getting used to the abode and all of just me,. He's even started to map out his territory by lying in the sun—a sign that he is getting spring/ summer excitement. I conclude saying: It was a nuisance yet recovery began happiness to my existence and the full treatment may be even more complete than beforehand. I lament over my loss of dad and the loss of our relationship. I kind of feel like I had been raised twice. The authority clean up from the grand larceny was wrapped up, concluded, and I never had a legal defense because the state took control and care of everything It was a shock. The man who was arrested and did four months in jail was my ex-pal Tony. I was relieved by all this neighborhood non-sense that it was over since moving away from Spring lake ranch, I left with gladness and never looked back. The girl Dawn was out of my life and for good. One good fact was that I never had to enter a courtroom. In my mind through this extra lover affair I wanted to wage a war with

Dawn's family, not the kids just the adults. Truely, I only think that I am a peaceful and humble person. On the other hand, here I am alone and sometimes lonely, but not struggling with "attitude is 90% of life. It takes two to discover another person and a self attitude (maybe towards that person). There are a few things I do for myself and feel quite proud of them, They were of coarse extracurricular in nature. For today I choose my own direction. The future may change my solitude. I am amazed to discover just the numerous government subsidized houses that occupy people like myself did for many years in Springfield Massachusetts and all over the tristate area. I have the utmost respect for Helen because she pulled me through most of the journey. I am toying with an idea to take on some additional employment and I got and applied to a new potential employer for supplemental work with a new boss and we meet over an interview to discuss shop talk. I spell out my usual routine to him. I live everyday with full energy and attending to business and enthusiasm. I pay rent with care and diligently, I wash clothes down in a common room, load a dishwasher upstairs, and the outdoor chores are outsourced by landscapers. I'll walk to the post office, then to the bank to take care of some financial stuff on pleasant days but the walk can be a little tough on my feet because its three miles away. I didn't continue with that job application, it'd be too much for me. The yard has peony petals still on the flowers. I grow a vegetable garden with cherry tomatoes and eggplants. Through that prior first employed job, I kept my car road worthy which had been one great feat. I had over 225,000 miles on that Hyundai before it went to the grave (alternator crapped out) but as for the new car, Damn! I am glad and lucky. The new car, the 2014 Honda, I keep mechanically well. I don't have a burning desire to travel like I used to. I learned the basics of automobile maintenance from these two: Jason and Bill. As I am always seeking an opportunity, I am of retirement age and it is better to realize its not how much I make its how I spend it. I put myself first, with that recent payday I fill up the cars tank and treat myself to a haircut.

* * *

It is a great place, the new apartment housing in Southold. If more complicated problems arise, I won't fix it alone. There are maintenance people on duty, My priorities are getting more situated now that I am saving on a real good path. If the car gives me problems I leave it to the experts. In the new diggs, I am in more pleased control. I do have to rely on credit sometimes, but what a great feeling to see into a landscape of independence and be away from a house of fifty or so unreliable, disoriented people. The co-op is out, it was sold and it's gone. It is now only a memory. Finally, there is no issue with modicum dwellings. It is a place just mine and. I am carrying on the embellishment and engaging at what I do at work in the Pilgrim state place job. Jim is dressing differently. He wears preppy clothes (the clothing line) on occasions. There is a stitch in time to fill. What is the clothing style for 2020? Next morning with early sunrise I first awoke to the regular routine. Some of my recent achievements, such as growing a propagation among mankind's natural spirit have been surfacing. "Make up the bed" Save the nine lives for boo boo. I am empowering my life but what I need is to love myself more. It is a Sunday and I hear a dog bark outside. That dog loves me more than I love myself. At a Sunday mass I walk up to take communion feeling proud, I am a foot taller than the whole congregation of (5'5"-average) and what a proud and a good feeling. Afterwards, I decided to cook baked potatoes. I put them in the oven at 325 and waited around my living room getting a little bored. I'd had enough of tv and puttering around and picking up, doing dishes, and cleaning. I got up and decide to fish. I went to a familiar spot and stayed there 45 minutes without a catch. I then drove along the road looking for another fishing spot. At that point I passed a firehouse, saw a red fire truck out of the corner of my left eye! "OH shit!" It joggled my head that I'd left the potatoes cooking in the apartment. I rushed home and things were safe. I take out the trash, bathe, clean the teeth, when I put out all the necessities' I need for the day ahead. On the day when I lost that safety net in college my head was really off keel and being tossed around like a sail boat in a storm. Thankfully I had been nurtured back to a commonality with society and able to have friends and able to respect myself. Most importantly I still have some family. After two parental lessons, my third stage is maybe I can marry. I am sure it was my personal music direction that screwed me up then. I deal with my equilibrium, ups and downs some days are, sullen and other days are happy. Some tasks are illuminating and sometimes things are boring. I won't ever feel the way again I had at college: stuck in a deep pit and unable to crawl out of it to the surface. aka I call that depression. I remember I had one apartment there in college that was overflowing with clothes strewn all over and garbage everywhere. The pressure of college can be so acute but when my safety net collapsed I was hung up. Pushing the flow of those mournful tears away becomes a real excitement for the future In conclusion, I had a bad track record of prior work. I work on my ethics today: improve self-esteem. Heck, living in a quiet atmosphere of amber is better than a dead atmosphere. The Spring lake ranch residence was a dead atmosphere. The work is security. Shaping the future with a long range goal, but aware of the kick back like one throws a boomerang out into the air, the unfortunate events of my early college are too far in the past to resurface. It will never be thrown back at me. Theres no magic success with just a diploma. Even Grandpa Young said that "with that college degree and a bus token I could get a ride on any bus." Investing and insuring can be on my list but there are drawbacks still in my life that I can't attend to the stock market, investing, etc. I juggle the bills every month and my managerial accounting is improving. "See Dawn again?" Don't God forbid that! (genisis). Wasn't it a bite from the plum That sent mankind spiraling downward. Tomorrow the dawn will definitely rise. Whether I see it or not or whether no one here gets out alive God is always.

Holy wonders, the world is not how I envisioned it to be today since that one day in the psychiatrist's chair that was the straw that broke the camel's back! As I look back at my rearing as a kid now and then I can almost laugh at this unfolding of my own myth: as it could be....I keep up with my dowsing searches. I keep evil away. I am always aware of my own time, people and places. I simply want to get out of this handicap of myself.

6:14 a.m.

The banged up silver, 2014 Honda Accord sat parked in my spot, albeit it was drivable and I used it only to and from work at the Pilgrim State Psychiatric hospital, The front Windshield was smashed. A rock was thrown through it. With my housekeeping job in the hospital I was responsible to be signed in and at work by six am. For most of the calendar year it meant being there before the dawn sunrise, yet in summer months or until early September the sun was up, I am 65 and single, after a bad love romance with Dawn: A narcissist girl of 35. I am happier to be alone in this abode of my simple nature. I am almost always in my home. Someone was going to be capsulated.

****

She'd knocked on my door and rang the bell for one hour straight from 3 am to four. When she finally yelled "I want my phone back" I went to the door to give her the phone. She began to wrestle me, so I gave her a right in the jaw, she fell backwards. Then she got up but I'd gotten into my home and locked the door. As children we. ve all been witnesses to domestic violence, and it's all over tv. This was unfortunate.

And I am remorseful. My finances were not enough for her demands. She was mentally ill on a deeper level. She was a kleptomaniac, that: no sane health Professional wants to attend to. My payments are doable, reasonable and all the years I have lived here. Damn she was so manipulative and a substance abusing /in and out of rehabs many times, and never coming clean. I had my number changed to protect myself with privacy, This didn't work many times She was not doable. I make my life with the income I have and I don't require a significant other. Its just not affordable. The Honda was repaired on the weeks ahead Insurance took care of everything and it had the look and feel of an A1 car again. Everyday I am conscientious that I was troubled by that Dawn, I keep on the lookout that I will not cross her path again. inside at work the job requires a lot of cleaning and after when I get home the routine encourages me for the house to clean as well These present days are chock full of a commencement to spiritual well-being, a time for myself, it is like my retirement yet I still work, I have been at this job for two full years, My social security disability income was dropped but in less than a year away I am eligible for retirement income. As I reflect on my long ago very fun and sheltered childhood I see more of reality, I am very proud of who I've become. One mishap In the incremental health growth, awe awe. I was reared in a very good family, one that emphasized recreation and not a heavy look at ethics. Here in Long Island the atmosphere is new and different and so the diversity in Long Island shocked, me. The street smart, manipulative personas I keep my eyes on for what is in front of me. I have run into some that don't share the bread in a retroactive positive light. I am trying upward mobility. With the changing world: Because of the declivity of government housing after-care I looked deeply inside. And I waited for this apartment for over twelve years. I will upscale my own well being. Just ME! Once an acute illness is under some stability our patient has $1000 dollars per month to live with and even in insurance licensing they quote "living on social security disability is a fate worse than death," As my founding family once said about Calvin Coolige's quote: "Nothing is certain except death and taxes." I had aspired to at least be a high income business executive.

Epithet

God is the creator to trust. Our universe is full of good and evil. It is an almost awesome world we live in But it falls way, way short. Its people that can be ugly.

www.ingramcontent.com/pod-product-compliance
Lightning Source LLC
Chambersburg PA
CBHW051217120626
46547CB00013B/1395